THE CARE OF THE AGED

There are today nearly four times as many old people in this country as at the beginning of the century. Their numbers, in comparison with other age groups in our society, have never been higher in any period of history. In recent years the care of the aged has become a serious social problem, arising by sheer weight of numbers as more and more old people are being kept alive by an ever-widening range of antibiotics to cure disease, by better surgery, better hygiene, more balanced diets, and warmer homes.

How best can we meet the claim of old people to the care and attention which is their birthright? A generation ago, grandparents were—at least in the absence of a chronic illness—traditionally looked after by the younger members of the family unit. Now when a grandparent goes into hospital with pneumonia, the family is often reluctant to take her back, even when she has made a perfectly good recovery. In this book Dr. Dennis Hyams, a Consultant Physician in charge of the Guy's Hospital Department of Geriatric Medicine, challenges our attitudes to ageing and the aged, in the firm belief that the community and the family must *care*. In his Foreword Lord Amulree, the distinguished physician and parliamentarian, writes "This is a book of value to all those people, both medical and lay, whose work lies among the elderly".

But it is our duty, my young friends, to resist old age; to compensate for its defects by a watchful care; to fight against it as we would fight against disease; to adopt a regimen of health; to practise moderate exercise; and to take just enough food and drink to restore our strength and not to overburden it. Nor indeed are we to give our attention solely to the body; much greater care is due to the mind and soul; for they, too, like lamps, grow dim with time, unless we keep them supplied with oil. Moreover, exercise causes the body to become heavy with fatigue but intellectual activity gives buoyancy to the mind.

CICERO, 106-43 B.C.
De Senectute

THE CARE
OF THE AGED

DENNIS HYAMS
MB, BS, MRCP

Consultant Physician, Guy's Hospital
Department of Geriatric Medicine,
New Cross Hospital, London

Foreword by

LORD AMULREE MD(Cantab), FRCP(Lond)

Consulting Physician, University College
Hospital, London, and President of the
British Geriatric Society

TECHNOMIC PUBLISHING COMPANY

Contents

FOREWORD, Lord Amulree   7
PREFACE   11

1 THE ELDERLY AMONGST US
  Introduction   15
  Old Age   16
  The process of ageing   17
  Causes of ageing   19
  Can we live longer?   21
  An ageing population   23
  Ageing and the community   27
  Changes in healthy individuals   29
  Old and ill   33
  Daily living activities   50
  Maintaining health   51
  Attitudes to older people   60
    Individuals   62
    Relatives and friends   64
    The community   69
  Retirement   71
  Useful Addresses   74

2 A PRACTICAL GUIDE TO HELP AVAILABLE
  In the community   77
  In the hospital service   105
  HOW TO FIND HELP   113
  Useful Addresses   116

3 TOWARDS THE END OF THE ROAD
  Facing the inevitable   121
  Hostels for the dying   122
  Euthanasia—for and against   123

4 A LOOK TO THE FUTURE   131

The Care of the Aged

5 SOME TYPICAL SITUATIONS
   Management and mis-management   135
      Trivial causes of big problems   135
6 A NOTE ON THE ORGANISATION AND REORGANISATION
   OF HEALTH AND PERSONAL SOCIAL SERVICES   143
7 AIDS TO DAILY LIVING   145
   Dressing aids   147
   Kitchen gadgets   148
   Bathroom & W.C.   150
   General mobility   152
   Bed aids   153

   FURTHER READING   155
   INDEX   157

Foreword

by Lord Amulree, MD, FRCP

MY friend and former colleague, Dr. Dennis Hyams, has written a book, based on his own experience, which will be of interest and value to all those people, both medical and lay, whose work lies among the elderly. It is particularly useful to them to know of the various bodies, both official and voluntary, who are able to help them in their work.

While it must always be accepted that an elderly person, when ill, may need admission to hospital as do middle aged and young persons, the idea of permanent custodial care is now becoming increasingly regarded with horror and dismay.

The late Dr. Marjorie Warren, from whose imaginative and revolutionary work among the inmates of the chronic sick wards of the West Middlesex Hospital during the 1930s so much of the modern idea for the management of elderly sick persons has its roots, used to teach that the most dangerous place for an old person to be was in bed in a hospital and the second most dangerous place was in a hospital at all!

The alternative is for the elderly to spend as much of their time as possible in their own home. To attain this end there has been a big increase in the number of services which are available to help elderly persons, and

7

others, in their homes. One of the most important are the home helps who will clean, shop, light the fire and who often become a devoted friend of their elderly client. This service is provided by the local authority at a fixed hourly charge and in the case of pensioners this charge is often waived altogether.

Next in importance comes the meals-on-wheels service, which will supply an elderly person with a hot mid-day meal. Meals delivered to a home were at first provided by voluntary sources notably the W.R.V.S. and the B.R.C.S., but local authorities can now supply meals from their own sources. Again, there can be a fixed charge for this meal, but this is usually waived for pensioners. Most meal services only deliver a meal to any one person on two or three days a week. It is to be hoped that in time a six day service will be available for all who need a meal: this would greatly benefit many old people. Other services, including nursing, are also available and every effort should be made to keep elderly persons in their own homes: alterations to the house or flat can be carried out by the local authority, to remove awkward steps, etc. in a home, and a good council can be very helpful.

But adherence to the doctrine of maintaining an old person in her own home must be looked upon in an intelligent way. For example, is the life of a lonely, house-bound old lady, living under not very satisfactory conditions, whose only contact with the world is the visit of her home help, for one hour, on five or six days a week really a rewarding and satisfactory one? Might not she be happier living in a "sheltered housing" scheme? (This is a group of tiny flats, or bungalows, grouped on a single site with living quarters for a warden or care-taker); or even in an almshouse (that admirable form of sheltered housing that goes back to the middle ages).

It is always dangerous to get involved in dogma, for then the personality of the living person tends to be overlooked, if not forgotten.

Elderly people, when sick, in many cases respond to suitable and active treatment as well, and almost as quickly, as do their younger contemporaries and they should never be denied the benefit of such treatment. This they often are, on the plea of a long waiting list or of the fear that they may block an "acute" bed in a hospital. The authorities, whoever they are, should realise that hospitals are really there for the care of the sick, irrespective of age. Arrangements must also be available so that on discharge, if they are not considered fit enough to return to an independent life, they may enter some sort of sheltered housing, which will usually be provided by the local authority. But it is often the case that local authorities have not fulfilled completely their obligations under the National Assistance Act 1948 and accommodation is not available, with the result that the elderly person is forced to remain in the hospital to the distress of all concerned, including the patient.

The establishment of Social Service departments by the local authorities has received a rather lukewarm welcome, especially for those who are concerned with the welfare of elderly persons. It seems possible that by increasing the separation between what used to be called health and welfare, some of the elderly may escape from under the medical umbrella which has been sheltering so many of them for so long. It will be necessary for the officers of the new department to consult frequently with their medical colleagues on the problems and help required by elderly persons who do not obviously fit into a recognisable category of "sick," however disabled they may be, and who would benefit from expert medical advice and treatment.

Old age is something which concerns us *all* and we have a duty in helping to provide for the adequate care of old people. To this end Dr. Hyams' book makes a significant contribution.

London, May 1972   AMULREE

Preface

THIS book sets out to describe the ways in which the elderly and their relatives and friends may be aided to live more satisfying lives when problems loom. It describes the growth of the elderly section of the community and explains how old age brings various problems which require *informed management*—rather than just "treatment." The philosophy behind this management is set out and the practical aspects of obtaining the best results are outlined. The many sources of help are indicated, together with the means of obtaining them and some of the difficulties which may be encountered along the way.

A recent survey conducted in Wandsworth and Reading, and reported in the Consumer's Association magazine *Which?*, showed what it considered to be "a serious failure" of contact and links between the general practitioner and hospital services on the one hand and the local authority social services on the other. Many persons in need of assistance were not receiving it (a fact already well-documented by Peter Townsend and Dorothy Wedderburn*); yet most of these people were known to some medical person or department. It was found that the functions of local authority Departments of Social Services were only vaguely understood by the public, and there was still the suggestion of "social stigma" (asking

---

* Townsend, P., and Wedderburn, D. (1965), *The Aged in the Welfare State*, G. Bell and Sons.

for "charity" or showing "inadequacy") about seeking help from the "welfare." Clearly there is the need for much further public and professional education about these matters.

It is hoped that this book will help to fill the gap and that the sections considering the philosophical and factual background will add to its value for readers of all ages.

Acknowledgements

IT is my pleasure to thank the several members of my Geriatrics team who gave me helpful advice in the preparation of the manuscript, and Dr. Geoffrey Eley, of Priory Press Limited, whose patience and co-operation have been of great assistance to me throughout.

The line drawings were made by Mrs. A. V. Christie.

I

The Elderly
Amongst Us

Introduction

OLD age, like the air, is all around us. The numbers of old people in the population have been increasing for some time and will continue to do so for some years to come. In addition, the proportion of old people in the population has been rising for some years and has reached a very high level which will probably be maintained for the remainder of this century. These facts raise several questions. What is old age anyway? Why do we age? Why have old people increased in numbers and proportion over recent years and why will this trend continue?—and for how long? Why do they sometimes present problems to their relatives, friends and neighbours and to medical and social services? How big are these problems? How is the community as a whole affected? What is being done to help and what more can be expected in the future?

In trying to answer these questions, special emphasis will be placed on practical aspects of helping old people, and of making life easier for those who wish to try to help them.

Old age

"You don't grow old—when you cease to grow you are old."—C. J. Herrick.

Let us first consider some basic issues. What is old age? When can a person fairly be called old, and does it really matter anyway? Why do we age?

Old age is hard to define. It is simply the opposite of youth; but it is characterised by loss of adaptability and decreased survival capacity with the passage of time. There is no precise point at which we become old: but since we are concentrating on practical matters we need to know when to regard a person as old. Purely for convenience, we tend to use pensionable age as a dividing line between middle age and old age—i.e. 60 years in women and 65 years in men. There is now an increasing tendency to use age 65 in both sexes. This is convenient but has little real meaning, for what matters most is not the chronological age—(i.e. age in years) but the *biological* age—(i.e. the functional state of the living organism). We all know people of 55 say, who are clearly "old before their time", either in body or in mind, or both. We know, too, of the sprightly 80-year-old who is so alert and active as to defy the description "old" in the usual sense.

In other words, we all tend to use the word "old" and the term "old age" in a loose and often inaccurate sense. This results from the familiarity with old age as we see it around us, combined with a lack of clear thinking about it. That is why it is sometimes taken amiss to call someone "old", and one has to be very careful not to tread on toes! More important, we must try to avoid the term "senile". This word, more than any other, has done great harm to the image of old people in general and the way many people regard them. Chambers' English Dictionary defines senility as "the imbecility associated with old age". This is indeed an insult, and I take issue with it. "Senile" means "old" and nothing more; but it has acquired an emotive quality which associates it with something degenerate and irreversible. Many people think that "senile" implies "untreatable" and the result is that too many old people have been accepted as untreatable and have been left to suffer unnecessary ill health and hardship.

The term "senile" tends to close the door to rational thought about an old person, and should be avoided. As will be seen later, *an optimistic approach is essential when dealing with old people*; it often pays handsome dividends.

The process of ageing

What is this process of ageing which is so inevitable a stage in the latter part of life? It must be admitted that there is much that is not understood about this matter. Ageing, in the broadest sense, may in fact be considered to begin at conception. The newly created organism begins to grow and develop from the union of sperm and egg cell, and once it comes into being, its age increases. In other words, ageing is a type of change in living systems due to the passage of time.

This is not pedantic, because the processes of ageing are still largely mysterious and need to be studied from the earliest possible moment. The passage of time may be seen in different perspectives at different times of life— e.g., a nine-month-old baby has already doubled its life-span since it took nine months to develop in the womb before birth; the 25 years from birth to 25 are very different from the 25 years from 65 to 90.

However, to remain in the field of practical understanding I shall confine my remarks to ageing in later life ("senescence"). This ageing process, though continuous, often seems to occur in sudden bursts. A person may be considered to have "aged overnight". No one knows why these fluctuations and bursts occur, but their existence must be acknowledged. The net result is involution, i.e., a "shrinkage" or regression. The organs, tissues and cells of the body show losses of structure and function such that the balancing of normal life processes becomes more precarious. We may express this as a "loss of functional reserve" in the individual, so that a stress which could be coped with in younger days may become a hazard in later life, or may even produce disease. Disease must be distinguished from *degeneration*, which actually begins quite early in life but shows itself (or its effects) most obviously in later years. Thus, one form of arthritis (osteoarthritis) may be considered as degenerative; others —including rheumatoid arthritis and gout—are diseases. Doctors must distinguish between these because the implications of disease are different from those of degeneration. Yet the two often occur together in the elderly, which makes it more difficult to assess and manage an elderly patient; and severe degeneration may produce disease (literally, dis-ease).

For these and other reasons, the speciality of geriatric medicine has evolved and this will be considered in more detail later.

For the moment, we may confine ourselves to the concept that ageing brings degenerative processes inevitably, but not necessarily diseases. These degenerations may affect various parts of the body, notably the arteries (blood vessels carrying blood to all parts of the body), joints, brain, kidneys and lungs.

These changes will eventually affect the majority of

people, but in different degrees, and the resulting disabilities may be minor or major or anything in between.
Loss of vigour is the accompaniment of ageing.

To sum up, though ageing is inevitable, it may not of
itself produce significant changes in function, or at least
not for many years. This will vary with one's inheritance
and way of life, but the precise causes of the changes
which occur with ageing are unknown.

Nevertheless, it is clearly no insult to be called "old",
and is often merely a matter of convenience!

Further, degeneration is not disease, but may produce
some disability which needs to be considered separately
from disease processes in assessing the state of health and
functional abilities of an old person.

Causes of ageing

Although the causes of ageing are not known, many
theories have been put forward, and some exciting experimental evidence has been produced in support of
certain of them. It is impossible to go into the numerous
theories here, but one or two deserve mention.

(i) *Loss of cells with ageing.* Most of these cells are
specialised, particularly those of the brain. It has been
suggested that this process begins in the young adult and
continues throughout the rest of life. Since many such
specialised cells cannot be reproduced by the body, there
is a "wearing out" process—which is ageing. At the
simplest level, the changes are considered as due to simple
degeneration.

Variations on this theory try to explain the cell-loss
in terms of inborn or acquired changes in genetic material[1]

---

[1] Genes are storehouses of hereditary information present in all cells which
possess a nucleus—i.e., nearly all the cells in the body.

or loss of the cells' ability to "understand" the programme for its functioning as laid down in its genes.[1] One idea is that the body fails to recognise some of its own cells and attacks them as it would foreign cells as, for instance, when a graft or transplant is rejected.

(ii) *Changes in cell function* may thus precede cell-death, and may be due to energy changes within the cell, physical changes due to "cross-linking" between protein components within the cells, accumulation of mutations (random changes in genes) or of free radicals (toxic chemical substances) such as may be produced by radiation, or of some sorts of waste products which cannot be eliminated.

(iii) *Accumulation of errors in protein manufacture.* This is a popular theory with considerable experimental evidence to back it, although it is probably not the whole answer to the ageing process.

The genes are the site of complex biochemical processes which allow "copying" of various proteins vital to the function of the cells, the tissues, and the whole body. Some of these proteins are enzymes or catalysts which control most of the cell-chemistry; and under their influence other proteins are made which have important functions in the cell and outside it. If a chance error were to occur in the manufacture of the enzyme, the ensuing reactions and newly made proteins would be defective and a vicious cycle might be set up. More and more "wrong" catalysts would help produce more and more "wrong" proteins, and eventually the cell would fail and die. This is an important and fascinating concept and further experimental work is proceeding to provide more information on it and on ageing processes generally.

[1] See footnote on page 19.

Can we live longer?

"The art of living consists of dying young—but as late as possible."—(Anon).

For nearly half a century, it has been known that chronic under-feeding (though this does not mean malnutrition) can prolong the life of certain animals such as fish and rats. In view of the life-span of humans it is difficult to apply the technique to man on an experimental basis.

Attempts at "rejuvenation" by hormones, especially sex hormones, have long been discredited although such treatments still find favour in some circles. Apart from specific replacement therapy for diseases known to be caused by hormone deficiency, this type of treatment has no place in prevention or treatment of ageing. It has not been scientifically shown to have any effect on ageing processes and it may indeed do harm.

Recently a substance named H3 was advocated as an agent capable of reducing the rate and effects of ageing, and of prolonging life in animals and man. These claims emanated from Rumania, but the studies were inadequately controlled. Small-scale controlled trials were carried out in Great Britain, but showed no useful effects. H3 was, in fact, procaine—a well-known local anaesthetic, and it was given by injection. More recently, an oral form, KH3, has appeared and the oral preparation contains other factors besides procaine, but there is still no satisfactory scientific evidence that its use fulfils the claims made for it.

It is of interest, however, that several other compounds, which do seem to show some experimental evidence of increasing longevity in animals, have local anaesthetic properties.

One of the most promising classes of compounds which may increase animal longevity is known as anti-oxidants. One of these BHT (butylated hydroxytoluene) is used as an additive by the food industry to preserve fat in various products. Much larger doses were used in the experiments which prolonged the life of mice by half as much again as their normal lifespan.

Much more work needs to be done along these lines before such compounds can be tried in man, but the possibility of extending our lifespan is by no means remote. Some opinions have been expressed that a significant increase in human lifespan may be achieved within the next 50 years.

Of prime importance is the question of whether such potential increase in human longevity is desirable in a world beset with problems of overpopulation. However, before any notable effect could result in overall world population there would need to be significant advances in control of today's major problems of old age—including degenerative processes causing disability and diseases such as heart and brain thrombosis, and cancer. It has been calculated that even if arterial disease and cancer were completely eradicated the extra period added to life would on average be quite small—a few years at most.

Once these medical problems can be conquered, any real effect of increased longevity could become apparent; even then the total increase in world population would be relatively small.

It is worth pursuing research into ageing processes not just to try to increase human lifespan but because it must involve studies of metabolic events in individual cells and tissues, which may be very revealing for their own sake, particularly in regard to the understanding of mechanisms which may be deranged in the evolution of various disease processes—notably cancer.

An ageing population

"To be 70 years young is sometimes far more cheerful and hopeful than to be 40 years old."—Oliver Wendell Holmes.

It is worth considering the size of the problem and its trends. The average age of the population of the United Kingdom has doubled in the last 150 years. At present (1972), there are about $6\frac{1}{2}$ million persons aged 65 and over in the United Kingdom. This represents 13 per cent or just over one-eighth of the total population.

A century ago, these figures were 1 million (5 per cent) and it is estimated that by the year 1991 they will be over $8\frac{1}{4}$ million ($13\frac{1}{2}$ per cent). More details are given in the Table:

Year	Number of persons 65 and over	% of total population
1841	700,000	4.5
1861	900,000	4.8
1871	1,000,000	5
1901	1,500,000	5
1911	2,106,000	
1939	4,200,000	
1947	5,000,000	10.5
1966	6,400,000	12.5
1972	6,500,000	13

Predicted figures:[1]

1976	7,800,000	13.6
1981	8,141,000	13.8
1991	8,350,000	13.4
2001	8,086,000	12.2

This Table shows that during the twentieth century there has already been a greater than fourfold increase in the number of elderly, and Fig 1 shows that the rate of this increase has been much faster for the group aged 65 than for younger groups.

Fig 1 Population of England and Wales, by age, 1841 to 1961, and projections to 1991.
Source: 1961 census of England and Wales. Registrar General's Statistical Review of England and Wales, 1965, Part II.

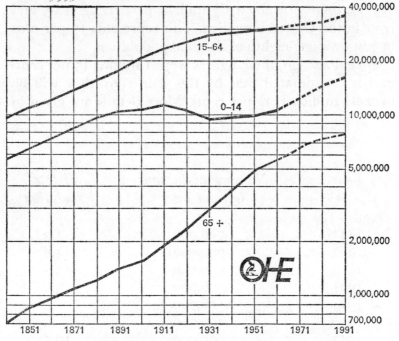

Note: Logarithmic scale.

[1] From the Registrar General's Office of Population Censuses and Surveys (1970).

24

This trend has been especially marked in the last 60 years and the Registrar General's figures for the projected future population show that the trend will continue until nearly the end of the present century.

We are now in a phase in which the increase of the oldest age groups is most remarkable, so that more and more persons are reaching an age in excess of 75 years. This process will continue into the twenty-first century; it is estimated that in 2001 there will be 3,464,000 persons aged 75 and over in the United Kingdom, as compared with 2,502,000 in 1969 and 2,228,000 in 1961. The number aged 85 and over rose from under 50,000 in 1901 to nearly 350,000 in 1961. It is estimated that the figure will be 500,000 by 1981, and 686,000 by 2001. Females aged 85 and over in 1991 will number twice as many as those in 1961.

There are several reasons which account for these dramatic changes.

(i) *Birth rates.* In 1881 there were 34 live births per 1,000 population. By 1941 the birth rate had fallen to 16 live births per 1,000 population. This was due to contraception and changes in economic standards with more women going out to work.

Clearly, there will be many old people alive now as a result of the high birth-rate of Victorian times, and they will represent a higher proportion of the total population in view of the subsequent decrease in birth rate. Equally clearly, this proportion will eventually start to fall, although there will be a further rise early in the twenty-first century when those individuals born in the "baby-boom" following the Second World War reach retirement age.

(ii) *Death rates.* These have decreased in the last 70

years, but it should be realised that the improvement has affected mainly children and young adults. This improvement is due to medical advances involving the control of infections—such as tuberculosis, pneumonia and epidemic diseases—by public health measures and antibiotics, improved maternity care with marked decrease in infant mortality, improved standards of living and better occupational health measures. As a result, more and more younger people have been preserved to reach old age. These medical advances have not made comparable improvements to the length of life of people already old: the expectation of life at the age of 60 is not much more than it was a century ago; the mean expectation of life at 80 is probably *less* than in 1872, since at that time a person surviving to 80 had to have a strong constitution, whereas now many 80-year-olds are frail and have survived to that age by virtue of the preservation of life at younger ages.

The overall lifespan has not been significantly increased; but the expectation of life at birth has risen for males from 44 years in 1891–1900 to 68.6 years in 1964.[1] In recent years, death rates among women have fallen faster than among men, so that life expectancy for females is higher than for males—in 1964, expectation of life for a newborn girl was 74.7 years.

(iii) *Effects of migration.* These are not marked in Great Britain as a whole, but have interesting effects in particular localities. For instance, many south coast resorts are favoured for retirement and the elderly living there represent at least twice the national average percentage of aged in the population. In other words, 25–30 per cent of the population of south coast resorts are 65 and over. Similar considerations apply to rural or underdeveloped

[1] *Registrar General's Statistical Review of England and Wales for the Year 1964*, Part I, H.M.S.O., London. (1966).

areas where the young move away to seek employment elsewhere, leaving a relatively high percentage of the old.

In countries such as U.S.A., Canada, Australia and Ireland the age structure of the population is more influenced by migration.

Ageing and the community

The increasing numbers and proportion of the elderly are being supported by a decreasing proportion of persons of working age. At present, there are about four persons of working age to one pensioner, whereas at the beginning of the century the ratio was 12 : 1. It is reckoned that there is one elderly person to every married couple over 45. But at 45 most couples are just beginning to be freed of responsibility for their children and could begin to enjoy a little more freedom and if an elderly relative now becomes dependent upon them—and especially if she moves in to live with them—new problems and frustrations easily arise.

At the age of 75 and above, there are twice as many women as men living, and two out of three of these elderly women are widows. There are 2,000,000 widows and half a million widowers aged 65 and over in Great Britain today. There is inevitably an increase in people living alone, and this may lead to varying degrees of "aloneness", as described by Tunstall[1] :

> *Living alone*—adequately and perhaps from choice.
> *Social isolation*—lack of social or family contacts.
> *Loneliness*—a subjective *feeling* of being lonely. This is not necessarily related to actual or social isolation;

[1] Tunstall, J. (1966). *Old and Alone—a sociological study of old people* (Routledge and Kegan Paul, London).

27

one can be lonely in a crowd or in a residential home. It is important, because it frequently leads to trouble in old age; loneliness may lead to apathy which in turn leads to self-neglect and loss of self-respect. These can have far-reaching consequences in terms of physical and mental health in old age.

Anomia—a withdrawal from normal social values in society. This may be the extreme result of the process described in the preceding paragraph, age is likely to affect men more often than women.

Aloneness is especially likely to be found in the single, the recently bereaved and the housebound or disabled. Lack of relatives, or of concern by relatives, and enforced retirement are also potent causes of social isolation.

As explained earlier, there will be a preponderance of old ladies in the elderly population. In fact, the excess increases in each of the eighth, ninth and tenth decades. Since ill-health is commoner in elderly women than in elderly men, large numbers of elderly women will require assistance from their families and from medical and social services; old men present a far smaller problem.

Disability increases markedly with age, with a sharp rise after the age of 60. Of persons aged 80, about one tenth are invalids and half of this age group have some impairment of health.

For all the reasons outlined, the elderly make great demands on medical and social services. Nearly a third of the expenditure on the National Health Service is directed towards those of 65 and over—a group representing only 12–13 per cent of the population.

Hospital wards in many specialities often have 50–70 per cent of their occupants aged 65 and over. Of course, some increase in demand is to be expected with increasing age; but the actual figure is much larger than might have been predicted. However, only 2–3 per cent of old people are in hospital; 97–98 per cent are in the community (2–3 per cent in residential homes and about 95 per cent in private dwellings). The load placed upon relatives, family doctors, district nurses and other community services is, as seen from these figures, enormous.

Changes in healthy individuals

"If you want to be a dear old lady at 70 you should start early, say about 17."—Maude Royden.

Bodily changes. Although some growth continues in old age—including the replacement of skin and blood cells—the main trend is the involution or regression already referred to. I have also described the progressive loss of irreplaceable specialised cells in the ageing body and mentioned the way in which this leads to a loss of reserve capabilities and a loss of adaptability to sudden or sustained stresses. The cells are replaced by inactive supporting tissue. The composition of the body changes so that there is less water and more fat in the elderly body as compared with the young one. There is a decrease in "lean cell-mass", or actively metabolising tissue, since fat is metabolically relatively inert compared with, say, muscle. The extra fat is not to be found under the skin, although there may be an excess here in obese old persons, but actually in the organs and tissues.

The skin becomes lax, perhaps wrinkled, and less elastic; changes occur in its supporting fibrous tissue. More pigmentation and "warts" may appear, and spontaneous bruising may occur, especially on the backs of the fore-arms and hands. Though muscle bulk may diminish, its strength does not necessarily fall very much. Hand-grip is often a good index of muscle power generally. Movements may be slower and more deliberate.

Height may be lost, usually due to postural changes, and a loss of weight is common after middle age.

Bones become thinner and more brittle, and degenerative changes occur frequently in some of the joints, though in a healthy old person these will not impair normal function.

The lungs become less elastic and less efficient in their task of providing oxygen for the blood. Altitudes may be less well tolerated than at younger ages.

The blood itself is usually formed normally, and anaemia is *not* a feature of normal ageing.

The healthy heart does not alter significantly but again there may well be diminished reserve capacity when extra stresses are added. The arteries show various changes, and the borderline between degeneration and disease may be most difficult to delineate here. Once there is impairment of blood flow in arteries sufficient to cause changes in the organs and tissues which they supply, those organs and tissues may be considered diseased—there is a deficiency of nutrients being brought via the blood, and secondary changes occur in the organs concerned. Thus may "coronary thrombosis" or "stroke illness" occur.

The stomach shows some changes in function, especially loss of acid in the gastric juice, but digestion and absorption of foodstuffs proceed virtually normally. The liver shows little or no change.

The kidney functions less well in the elderly but there is usually adequate reserve.

Glandular function declines somewhat, and this was

formerly thought to be a causal feature of ageing, but this is no longer accepted, and hormone treatments are not required or beneficial in the healthy old person. (This is not to deny that menopausal women, whose ovarian function is diminishing, leading to "hot flushes", etc. may benefit temporarily from small doses of female sex hormones.) The prostate gland enlarges in the male.

The brain shares in the progressive loss of cells over the years, and these cells are irreplaceable. Some loss of intellectual function, especially loss of recent memory, is so common in the elderly as to be almost the rule but in a healthy old person it is of no significance. It is helpful to recall some of the great works of art which were created by octogenarians—including Verdi's Otello and Falstaff, Goethe's Faust, paintings by Picasso and Miró.

Special senses tend to suffer in old age. Some eye functions even begin to diminish from the age of forty, and near-sightedness in old people is common. The common incidence of cataract and other eye diseases is acknowledged but they are not strictly part of normal ageing.

The ear also begins to show losses in function from about 40 years of age, but the healthy old person is not deaf for normal purposes of conversation.

Pain sensibility may decrease so that illness is often obscured for a longer time.

The old person has an easily disturbed body temperature and can adapt less well to climatic variations.

The general metabolism does not change but the total food needs of the elderly are less than those of younger subjects. On the other hand, there is less margin of adequacy in the diets of the elderly and nutritional deficiencies may appear more readily, especially in those living alone.

Psychological changes

(a)   *Intellectual changes*. Some loss of intellectual function has been mentioned as a very common finding in old
age, though often of no practical importance.

Intelligence tests may show some falling off, but this
depends on the type of tests used. Verbal and factual
knowledge tests do not tend to fall off, whereas abstract
reasoning or coping with new ideas may produce difficulties. This is due to slowing of brain-functions, more difficulty in learning new material and keeping it in store
to be drawn on when required, and generally a slowness
in mentally "changing gear" and moving on from one
topic to another.

Loss of recent memory is the commonest change. It
is often slight and may pass unnoticed, but may lead to
changes in behaviour and personality—for example, re-
petitive conversation is due to forgetting what has just
been said, and in more marked instances the person may
forget where she is or what time of day, month or year
it is and thus appear confused when in other matters a
person is certainly *not* confused. Similarly, a tendency to
live in the past is explained by the fact that memory for
distant events is well-preserved even though an old lady,
for instance, may forget what she has just eaten for break-
fast. This kind of forgetfulness can lead to domestic or
other personal difficulties where relatives become irrita-
ted by repetition of stories or other conversation, or by
the old lady who constantly loses her glasses and accuses
others of moving them or hiding them, or by the constant
stream of "good advice" offered and based on experiences
in younger years. This can be very tricky where young or
teenage children are involved in the domestic scene.

(b)   *Personality changes*. There is a lack of flexibility

32

and increased rigidity of outlook, so that some resistance to new ideas is common in old age. Interests narrow, emotional responses diminish, and there is a tendency to be concerned with self and less interested in what other people think. There may be a fierce spirit of independence. There is an exaggeration of earlier personality traits, so that a mean person may become a miser, a "loner" (or shy person) a hermit or tramp, and a "thorny" personality may become obstinate and difficult.

Preoccupation with the body may lead to an hypochondriac state—especially concern over bowel function and sometimes food fads. One elderly man I know habitually eats quantities of sunflower seeds because he claims to have heard of some Bulgarian research suggesting that this would prevent trouble from an enlarged prostate gland!

These changes as described might make a bleak impression on the reader; but they may in fact contribute to the role of the elder in society. The independence, avoidance of demanding relationships, conservatism and wisdom and humour derived from earlier years all help to adapt old people for their role as grandparents or family advisers or just plain good friends, at a time of their lives when they are best suited to these functions. However, there is a narrow margin between the satisfactory fulfilment of such a role and the real problems presented when disease processes add their weight to the delicate psychological balance.

Old and ill

"Idleness and the bed are the two pall-bearers of the living aged."—(Anon).

33

This chapter is concerned with the special problems which beset people who become ill when they are elderly. As we have shown, there is loss of reserve capacity in old age, so that old people become ill more readily than younger persons. It may also take longer to achieve recovery of *function* (which allows a reasonably independent existence) although recovery from a particular illness such as pneumonia or stroke may take no longer than in young patients. There are often other factors operating in the elderly, such as the frequent co-existence of several disabilities, which may impede progress.

Invalidism. The proportion of invalids increases steadily with age, and figures have already been given to illustrate this trend.

Multiple disabilities. Troubles rarely come singly to the old. It is the rule rather than the exception that multiple disabilities co-exist in individual elderly patients. The "fit" old person will have degenerative processes operating in many parts of the body, but compensates for their effects, and functions adequately. In the ill old person some disease is added to these processes, and/or some of the degenerative changes may become severe enough to cause disabilities in their own right. The result is a patient in whom the interplay of these forces of ill health will determine the precise functional capacity and the feasibility of applying appropriate treatments most effectively. For instance, an uncomplicated "stroke" calls for intensive rehabilitation which requires considerable effort on the part of the patient. If he has had in addition a "heart attack", or if he has suffered from severe arthritis or has had a previous leg amputation, his rehabilitation is going to be more difficult and more prolonged. Or perhaps the new stresses and strains brought about by the paralysed limbs may aggravate an arthritis hitherto compensated for, and this may create problems in managing the patient. Often there are social problems too; home conditions may require much modification before the patient can function adequately at home once more, even if he lives with relatives.

Silent illnesses. Many old people do not manifest the typical symptoms and signs which doctors expect to find in various illnesses. Many characteristically painful illnesses may be painless in the elderly; symptoms may be totally absent or quite other than anticipated; they are often very vague or "non-specific". Coupled with the fact that old people often do not come forward with their complaints, attributing many symptoms erroneously to old age, it can be seen how difficult it may be to establish precisely just when an old person really is ill, and what the illness is. Problems of communication (see below) add to the problem. Diagnosis of disease and disability is therefore all too often made later rather than early; and it is thought that there is much undiscovered disability in the elderly as a whole—the so-called "iceberg" phenomenon referred to later in this book.

Problems of communication. With the gradual loss of special senses, vision and hearing decline with ageing and there is increased difficulty in communicating with other people. A stroke illness may often affect the speech and thought mechanisms of the brain ("aphasia"), and in some cases this can produce great frustration in the patient, his relatives and helpers. Such a patient may find it difficult to make the best use of his remaining functions since learning skills (or re-learning old ones), and grappling with new situations, will be much harder for him. In considering speech defects after certain types of stroke, it is important to remember that patients who are left unable to speak intelligibly may still understand much or all of what is said to them. It is essential to speak normally (though carefully and clearly) to these patients, even though the conversation may appear at first to be one-sided. Questions answerable by "yes" or "no", or signs indicating yes or no, are the most helpful.

Aphasia may be associated with defects of reading, writing and calculating and sometimes defective performance of familiar movements or acts such as dressing or feeding—quite independently of the extent of actual muscle weakness. But just as many such patients understand spoken words and commands, so they may be able to read written questions or instructions. However, the difficulty of expressing their thoughts and meanings may present enormous problems. Every opportunity should be taken to encourage speech practice, using spoken and written words, and pictorial symbols in association with them. For further information, consult the Chest and Heart Association, Tavistock House North, Tavistock Square, London, WC1H9JE. This organisation publishes several useful items for those concerned with stroke patients: Nursing the "Stroke" patient (leaflet); Return to Independence (book of exercises); A Word and Picture Chart for aphasic patients; and a book setting out holiday addresses for patients who have had strokes or chest or heart problems.

Mental confusion. The brain of the older person is more easily clouded by all kinds of illness. The new appearance of confusion in a previously mentally clear old person is one of the commonest indications of physical bodily illness. It is akin to the delirium which may be seen in younger patients who are seriously ill, but in old people it occurs much more readily and much more often. One must not think that sudden confusion in an elderly person is due to a mental illness by itself; physical illness must be looked for diligently, because in such cases the mental changes are quite reversible once the underlying organic illness is successfully treated.

Apart from illnesses due to disease, drugs may be the cause of mental confusion. Old people react differently to drugs as compared with younger people, probably because their bodies handle the drugs less efficiently. Drugs (e.g. barbiturates) which are well-tried reliable remedies earlier in life may produce an acute confusional episode in an old person; occasionally other ill effects are noted.

It is a common error to regard as "confused" an old person whose major problem is intellectual loss, or dementia. Such persons have loss of recent memory which makes them forget who or where they are, or what they are trying to do, or where they have put things, or what time of day, week, month, year or even century it is. This causes them to be confused to some extent; but a significant degree of confusion is another matter, and may occur in the intellectually normal as well as demented subjects, given the appropriate circumstances as outlined above. Confusion implies a cutting off from reality and the significance of persistent confusion is very different from that of dementia. Some idea of a confused state may be gained from one's own experience when, emerging from a shop in a strange town, one realises that all sense of direction has been lost; or when day-dreaming; or when waking up during the night and, for a few moments, failing to realise just where one is. At such times the environment fails to make sufficient or appropriate impression upon one, and full reality is lacking. These episodes of confusion are, happily, brief but it is possible to imagine some of the problems one would face were they to persist.

Restlessness may result from physical discomfort, especially in patients who cannot fully appreciate what is happening, or in those who cannot communicate. An overloaded bowel or distended bladder may be the cause of restlessness. Occasionally, restlessness is due to a mental illness such as the manic-depressive state.

Aggressiveness may be found in the bully at any stage or in an irritable personality who has undergone some inhibition of higher mental processes due to ageing or brain damage—after a stroke, for instance. Some degree of aggressiveness can be of value to the patient by assisting his motivation to work hard at his rehabilitation. Too much aggression, however, is harmful to the patient himself, and may produce feelings of frustration too readily, preventing proper co-operation with the rehabilitation team and thus impeding his progress. Such patients are often more aggressive to their relatives than to their doctors, but this is not always the case. Occasionally, the aggression is part of a psychiatric illness, and there are *other disorders of behaviour* which may call for psychiatric help, e.g., those resulting from delusions of persecution.

Depression is common in the elderly but is very amenable to treatment in most cases.

Hazards of illness. Ill old people are especially likely to develop complications which are seen less frequently in the young.

Thus, *bedsores* may occur very readily in old people who are immobile or inert. They are due to pressure, especially shearing strains between a bony prominence and the overlying skin. They develop more commonly in hospital patients than in patients at home, and more often in general medical and surgical wards than in geriatric wards, where the staff are particularly aware of the problem.

Although they develop rapidly they may take weeks or months to heal and are a good illustration of the old saying that prevention is better than cure.

Another undesirable complication is the *contracture* of a joint—the joint loses some or all of its range of movement, and may become fixed in an abnormal position. This may be seen in diseases of the joint, for instance arthritis, or when some of the muscles moving the joint are weakened.

In the case of arthritis the joint may be kept in one position to give ease from pain; and it may become unable to resume the former range of movement once it stiffens up. This can occur surprisingly quickly. With muscle weakness, the stronger muscles put the joint into certain positions in which it may become fixed. Such a situation is sometimes seen after a stroke, where the arm on the affected side may be held closely to the chest due to contracture of the shoulder joint. Attempts to move the arm outwards or forwards will then meet with much resistance and may cause much pain to the patient ("frozen shoulder"). Such a patient may also show a bent elbow, dropped wrist, and approximation of the fingers on the affected side.

The knees may readily become fixed, and it is most important that full extension be preserved—that the legs can be fully straightened—otherwise the ablity to walk will soon be lost. This is especially important in patients with arthritis of the knees.

Prevention is again much easier than cure, and is

achieved by putting joints at risk through a full range of movement several times a day—passively if necessary, or by active movements wherever possible, giving such assistance as may be required.

Incontinence is common in the elderly patient, and needs detailed consideration. It is by no means always the intractable problem that many people imagine, but needs a commonsense appraisal and attitude on the part of all those who find themselves concerned with it. Many old people who are incontinent are extremely embarrassed by it, and it is a burden to those caring for the patient whether at home or in hospital. Incontinence has been termed the "thief of self-respect".

It is necessary to consider incontinence of urine and of faeces separately.

Just because a patient wets her clothing or bedlinen it does not follow that she has no control over her bladder. Certain factors must be considered from the start, such as the presence of urgency, If one tries to delay passing urine once the "call" has come, after a time much discomfort is experienced and this gets worse as time goes on. (Most of us will have experienced this!) Old people tolerate this delay less well, yet are more likely to experience delay—due to poor mobility (arthritis; after a "stroke" etc) and/or a lavatory at some distance, such as down the garden or up the stairs. Or in a busy general hospital ward an elderly patient may be kept waiting if nurses are busy. Incontinence of urine is a possibility in these situations. It has been stated that old people have only about two minutes from noting an urge to pass urine to loss of ability to hold it any longer. This means that the W.C. should not be more than 30-40 feet away at any time. The value of a commode or urine bottle in this situation is apparent.

An infection in the urine is common in old people, especially old ladies, and may lead to urgency and also to frequency, so that incontinence of urine is again more likely. The production of large volumes of urine may also predispose to urgency, frequency and incontinence.

Such incontinence has clearly delineated causative factors which can be readily dealt with, resulting in a continent patient.

Stress incontinence may occur on effort—a rise in pressure in the abdomen leading to a leakage of urine from the bladder. This has most commonly a gynaecological cause, such as a dropped womb in a woman who has borne several children many years before. It is often controlled by insertion of a ring pessary. Occasionally an operation is advised. The condition is seen in quite young women, too.

Overflow incontinence of urine occurs secondary to distension of the bladder, so that *retention of urine* may be the underlying cause of *apparent* incontinence. The retention may be due to obstruction of the normal outflow of urine from the bladder. An enlarged prostate gland in the male is a common cause of such obstruction. A similar type of enlargement of glandular tissue at the outlet or "neck" of the bladder in women may have similar results. Constipation may lead to so much distension of the rectum that bladder function is disturbed and retention of urine results, and again this may appear as "incontinence of urine". Sometimes a ring pessary worn by a woman with a dropped womb may interfere with bladder function and produce retention of urine and overflow incontinence; but more often such a pessary is used with good effect to control stress incontinence.

All the above causes of urinary incontinence are remediable and so the outlook for making the patient continent is good.

Diseases affecting the spinal cord and adjoining nerves may interfere with bladder function, but these are not common.

When all these factors have been ruled out, there still remain many patients with incontinence of urine which proves more difficult to control. This is believed to be due to brain damage, in patients with arteriosclerosis or after a stroke illness. In this situation, the normal control of bladder function is disturbed so that the bladder tends to empty as soon as it begins to fill—i.e., the bladder is small and over-excitable, leading to exaggerated waves of strong contractions of the bladder muscle, felt as urgency—or apparently not felt in time at all—so that the bladder empties too readily and too often. In this situation the "higher" controls by the brain (which prevent one passing urine at inappropriate times and inappropriate places) are missing or defective. The result may well be incontinence which is difficult to treat.

Even so, regular "toilet training" and possibly the use of drugs which relax the bladder muscle to some extent, may lead to the regaining of continence by the patient. This is aided by all possible measures to encourage self-respect in the patient—decent clothing, habits and accommodation—and to rehabilitate the patient.

In some patients incontinence of urine has been interpreted as part of a reaction against growing old—"let's be children again". Several features of some elderly patients suggest a retracing of the steps of childhood—

e.g. loss of walking ability; the need to be fed; lying curled up in bed—the bed being analogous to the womb and the urine to the fluid surrounding the unborn child.

Regression of this sort suggests the importance of psychological mechanisms and a New Zealand geriatrician draws an analogy between brain-washing techniques and some abnormal mental processes which might be seen in old age. Thus, it is known that normal behaviour patterns break down when stresses become too great; this is seen especially when resistance is lowered by fatigue, fever, drugs, glandular changes and ageing. Prolonged over-stressing leads to a protective mechanism in which normal responses are inhibited, and increasingly abnormal behaviour may ensue. The main feature is then paradoxical responses—i.e., the brain responds more actively to weak than to strong stimuli and this may vary and be unpredictable. Such features are seen in the patient who wets the bed as soon as the sheets have been changed, or the patient who refuses the commode and then wets herself, possibly striking out at her attendants at the same time.

Transfer of such patients to hospital leads inevitably to a degree of depersonalisation and loss of freedom, some regimentation, a new environment among strangers and poor communication. Breakdown of normal functioning occurs readily in such conditions. The best way to help is to encourage personalisation, with familiar objects and (as far as possible) people around, and the building-up of self-respect as indicated earlier. The more flexible is the hospital routine the more likely it is to help the elderly patient.

Frequent visiting by relatives and friends is of great value. But best of all is to avoid admitting the old person to hospital at all whenever possible, or, if unavoidable, to keep the admission as short as possible.

The outlook for combating urinary incontinence is worst where the patient does not seem to know or care that she is wet, which suggests appreciable deterioration in mental function. During re-training, or if these measures fail, incontinence pads may be helpful. They are often rather deficient in absorbing power, however, and need frequent changing. The new Gelulose[1] pad absorbs more urine than other types; it looks like a sanitary towel, and it is comfortable to wear and remains dry for long periods. Plastic pants keep in the moisture and the skin becomes wet, hot and uncomfortable; it may later become sore. A vastly better idea is to improvise pants from a sheet of "Marathon"one-way napkin material (knitted polypropylene). A piece of polythene is sewn over the region covering the genitals so as to make a pocket in which the absorbing pad can be placed. Ordinary underwear may be worn over these pants. In intractable cases, an appliance may have to be used, but leaves much to be desired, and is rarely feasible in women. The most difficult cases may require a catheter, left in the bladder, but changed at regular intervals. Ordinary catheters may need changing fortnightly but "Silastic" catheters may be left in for several months without being changed.

Night incontinence. In some instances there is incontinence of urine at night only; some incontinent patients regain bladder control by day long before night control is achieved. The same general principles of management are used, with special emphasis on the need for regular toilet training even during the night; the avoidance of heavy sleep (if necessary the patient should be awakened during

[1] Gelulose Products, 16 Dolphin Street, Manchester 12 6BG

the night to pass urine and possibly be given a bladder-relaxing drug) and perhaps the restriction of fluids in the evening and at night. Many "accidents" occur when the patient first awakens in the morning, so special viligance is needed at this time. Easy access to a bottle, commode, or W.C. is essential for the control of nocturnal incontinence.

Incontinence of faeces is usually due to a local cause in or near the rectum. Diarrhoea, due to excessive purgation or to bowel disorder, readily produces faecal incontinence in the elderly. One variety of diarrhoea, known as "spurious diarrhoea", is due to a leak of fluid around hard lumps of faeces packed into the rectum (impaction of faeces), as the result of chronic constipation. Thus incontinence of faeces may be due basically to constipation. This situation is quite common in old people. If this diagnosis is missed, a constipating remedy may be taken for the "diarrhoea", and this will merely aggravate the underlying problem. Occasionally a prolapsed (dropped) rectum is found in patients with faecal incontinence. An operation may then be required.

Less often, disease of the spinal cord and adjoining nerve leads to faecal incontinence. In a few patients brain damage—severe dementia, for instance—is associated with incontinence of faeces. Such cases will then have double incontinence—of urine and faeces—but if apparently incontinent of faeces only, a local cause should be suspected. Even a demented person may have severe constipation leading to spurious diarrhoea!

Constipation is very, very common in the elderly. But it is a term which means different things to different people. Some people believe they are constipated if they fail to open their bowels every day; yet a reasonably regular bowel action every two or three days may clear the bowel quite adequately and such persons would not be regarded by a doctor as constipated. On the other hand, some people who have a bowel action daily may still be constipated if they are having very incomplete evacuations (due to bad habits, laziness, dementia, unsatisfactory toilet arrangements, etc.).

Nevertheless, many old people *are* constipated and even more are convinced that they are. Preoccupation with the bowels is a common feature of old age.

The wall of the bowel is usually capable of adequate function even in old people, but in very frail and elderly subjects the bowel musculature may be weak. Weakness of the abdominal muscles may also be present, making it more difficult to strain at stool if the motion is hard. Inactivity in some aged persons will predispose to constipation.

The diet may contain too little "bulk", possibly on account of its expense or difficulties in chewing if teeth are poor or absent; or the subject may take too little fluid because of disinclination or fear of urinary difficulties. Ill old people frequently fail to show a normal thirst mechanism and may not take enough fluid unless their nurses remember to give them drinks without waiting to be asked.

Some of the more important results of constipation have been considered above—impaction of faeces, spurious diarrhoea with faecal incontinence, retention of urine possibly with overflow incontinence. Impaction of faeces may lead to restlessness and mental confusion and these may be the only clues to its presence. In severe cases, a degree of bowel obstruction may result.

In treating constipation, obvious contributory causes such as diet, fluid intake and bad habits, must be corrected.

Laxatives should be treated with respect. Liquid

paraffin is less desirable than was once thought, as it may be imperfectly swallowed and some droplets may find their way into the lungs and produce pneumonia; it may interfere with the absorption of certain vitamins from the food; and, passing unchanged through the bowel, it may leak out of the rectum.

Salts, such as Epsom or proprietary "fruit salts", act by retaining fluid in the bowel and so producing a soft stool; but they may easily produce a liquid stool with its difficulties and embarrassments, and the effervescence of the preparation may produce or aggravate a tendency to flatulence. However, many old people have taken a small dose of salts every morning for years and assert that this keeps their bowels regular. Others find that a glass of hot water first thing every morning is equally effective.

Another way of increasing "bulk" in the intestine is to administer an inert substance such as methyl cellulose or agar, which swells up on contact with liquid. If taken regularly, this may ensure regular bowel actions; but it may not appeal to the elderly as it is not always easy to take, and it has no quick and dramatic effects.

Stimulant laxatives actually cause contraction of the bowel wall, and are often necessary in old people—but must be selected with care. Strong stimulation is likely to purge and may produce incontinence of (liquid) faeces, and also produces colicky abdominal pains. "Vegetable laxative" may do this. Perhaps the most useful standby is standardised senna—e.g. "Senokot". Senna was formerly given as a "tea" brewed by infusing senna pods in cold water. This fails to produce a standard dose and has caused much trouble. "Senokot" is standardised so that the appropriate dose required for each person may be given each time, thus avoiding drastic purgation and

47

colic. Many elderly people have had daily or weekly laxatives since childhood, so that one is dealing with a really old-established habit here and treatment must be applied intelligently with this in mind.

To begin to clear the outlet, as it were, it may be necessary to use suppositories or enemas. In some severe cases of faecal impaction a manual removal of faeces has to be carried out by a nurse or doctor to allow the resumption of normal evacuations.

In prevention it is helpful to give regular doses of a special detergent which prevents the formation of hard lumps of faeces in the bowel. It has no purging action and is quite safe.

Low body temperature. Many old persons have a somewhat low "normal" body temperature. Although we usually say that the normal temperature is 98.4°F (37°C), it is not uncommon to find healthy old people with a temperature regularly in the range 95–96°F (35–35.6°C).

A proportion of old people are now thought to have defective control of their body temperature, so that in certain circumstances they lose body heat to an extent which can have serious consequences.

The obvious circumstance for this is low environmental temperature. A number of old people in Great Britain admitted to hospital in the winter months have body temperature below 95°F (35°C). This becomes serious when below 90°F (32.2°C) and especially if below 86°F (30°C). Such low body temperatures, known as hypothermia, are seen specially in newborn infants and old people in cold weather conditions. In the former, it is thought to be due to an immature body temperature-regulating mechanism and has even been recorded in the tropics. In the elderly, the mechanism has presumably become inefficient in certain individuals due to degenerative processes, or a cold environment is complicated by illness or disability in the old person.

A normal person—of any age—finds it unpleasant to feel cold and will take steps to overcome this—by putting on more clothes, warming the room, having a hot drink, or increasing his physical activity. If very cold, he shivers, which is an involuntary way of increasing muscle activity and so preventing a fall in body temperature.

Old people may not take appropriate measures to prevent or overcome this feeling of coldness—due either to illness which makes them feeble or unable to move (fractured thigh, "stroke", or loss of consciousness), to confusion or to poverty. In such instances a cold environment may lead to hypothermia.

The implication of this is that particular care needs to be taken in clothing and housing for old people, and heating should be adequate in even the coldest weather. Unfortunately, this is not always the case, for reasons which are not hard to find. The classical British cold bedroom is dangerous in old age. If necessary, an old person should sleep downstairs in a warm living-room rather than go to a cold bedroom for the night.

Each winter a room thermometer should be placed in sitting-room and bedroom. A temperature below 55°F is undesirable and one below 50°F is dangerous. Old people should be visited during cold weather. Prevention is vital; established hypothermia is dangerous.

Some drugs and various illnesses predispose to hypothermia. Immobility is also an important factor in some cases.

Hypothermia may also occur with normal environmental temperature. Apart from the predisposing factors mentioned above, sluggish thyroid gland function may allow the body temperature to fall too readily, even in a warm room.

If an old person is found unwell in a cold environment and feels cold to the touch even in covered parts of the trunk, he is probable hypothermic and medical attention should be sought at once. This is a medical emergency. It must be realised that an ordinary clinical thermometer may show a misleading body temperature in such a case, since it registers only down to 95°F (35°C), and such a reading does not exclude a still lower temperature. Even patients with a temperature of 75°F (23.9°C) will register 95°F (35°C) on such a thermometer since it cannot read any lower. A special low-reading thermometer which will read down to 75°F (23.9°C) is now carried by many doctors and district nurses and may be purchased from chemists.

It is most important to avoid local heat in such cases. Hot water bottles and electric blankets must *not* be used— such measures are too late and may be dangerous, even lethal. Whilst awaiting the doctor, warm the room so that warm air is breathed. If swallowing is normal, a hot drink may be given. The patient should be covered by one, or at the most two, blankets.

Daily living activities

It has been emphasised early in this book that therapeutic optimism is essential when dealing with old people. Likewise, an active approach to rehabilitation in the elderly is essential. This is well seen when an elderly patient is admitted to a geriatric department of a hospital for assessment and treatment. The physicians who work in such a department know that inactivity, and especially bedrest, is harmful for the aged, unless there are specific reasons for prescribing them. In most instances, the patient is treated out of bed, dressed in ordinary clothes, as soon as possible.

Walking is encouraged as it is a function very quickly lost in ill old people or even when confidence is lost after a fall or series of falls. Ordinary daily living activities are pursued as and when possible (feeding and dressing, washing and cooking, getting into and out of chair and bed, coping with doors, taps, levers and switches, toilet activities, and so on—see Chapter 7.) The aims are to preserve self-respect and promote independence whilst treating any illnesses or disabilities which might be tending to diminish these.

This dynamic approach sometimes puzzles or worries relatives, but it should be remembered that it is used because it has been shown to benefit the patient, although its intensity will vary from patient to patient according to need.

Before sending an old person home to live alone the daily living activities are again assessed to ensure that he will be able to cope with these basic tasks when at home.

Maintaining health

"The best physicians are **Dr. Diet**, **Dr. Quiet**, and **Dr. Merryman**."—Swift.

The avoidance of excesses, the flexing of physical (and mental) muscles, the acceptance of certain changes in bodily function, and the taking of special care in particular situations—all these will contribute to the maintenance of health in later life.

Avoidance of excesses. **Diet** should be well-balanced, with no less protein—meat, fish, eggs and cheese—than

in middle age, but with care over the intake of carbo-
hydrates such as sugar and starchy foods. The total daily
calorie (energy) needs are less than in earlier life. Vitamins
should be plentiful and fresh fruit and vegetables, bread,
milk and butter or margarine will provide these.

If obese, weight reduction should be pursued relent-
lessly. It is difficult for old people to diet, as food may be
one of their few pleasures, but obesity is the cause of so
much ill-health that every effort must be made to combat
it. Obesity predisposes to diabetes and aggravates the
problems of arthritis on weight-bearing joints such as hips,
knees, ankles. It is associated with gallstones, diseases of
the heart and blood vessels, and chest troubles. Obese
patients are more difficult to nurse, find walking more
difficult, and are more prone to complications after opera-
tions. They may develop skin rashes under pendulous
skin-folds or breasts.

Excesses of smoking and drinking speak for themselves.
Smoking is bad for lungs, heart and blood-vessels. Cigar-
ette smoking is more harmful than pipe or cigar smoking.
Alcohol in moderation may be beneficial in many ways,
especially as a night-cap or as a way of improving the
circulation in the feet and hands. But it is a foodstuff and
it is necessary to count its calories (as a carbohydrate) in a
diet for obesity or for diabetes. Spontaneous changes in
smoking and drinking habits may occur after middle age,
often due to financial restrictions; but it may be hard to
get an established habit changed in an old person. One
must question how hard in this situation one should try
to make such changes.

Heavy beer drinkers who give up the habit are likely
to find that they become constipated, due to the sharp reduction in fluid intake.

Habitual drinkers may "go off their beer" as a symptom

of an illness, and persistence of this symptom, in the absence of a deliberate effort to reduce intake, calls for a medical check-up.

Flexing the muscles. Activity of body and mind helps to preserve the function of both.

Physical exercise. Although loss of vigour occurs in old age, moderate exercise should be taken regularly and is beneficial in maintaining bodily fitness. Simple indoor exercises, or outdoor activity such as walking, gardening, cycling and swimming, or games and sports such as golf, bowls or fishing should be continued into the later years.

Mental activity. Losses occur least from well-trodden pathways: the "mental muscles" must also be flexed so that the mind is constantly working—by continuation of hobbies, crossword-solving, post-retirement jobs and such-like. The old person who spends the day idling is not in good mental health.

Acceptance of changes. Many of the losses associated with old age lead merely to diminution of *reserve* function; so that in ordinary use the various organs cope quite well and "normally". But lessened reserve powers mean the readier appearance of distress when extra strain is put on the body—so that, for example, the old person becomes breathless more readily and can tolerate less exercise than the younger individual. Constipation is common but, as explained earlier, means different things to different people. Special senses—taste and smell, vision and hearing—diminish to varying degrees.

Some of these losses can be compensated for—with, for instance, hearing aids, spectacles and dentures. Constipation can be treated and often prevented. But other changes occur which must be accepted—loss of vigour; tiring more readily; altered sleep pattern, with less sleep at night,[1] and some types of visual loss or hearing loss, are not amenable to treatment.

Care of the feet. This is important in the elderly, who often have impaired circulation to the feet; it is also important in diabetics. In all these subjects, minor injury to the feet, or overheating the feet, can lead to major problems. Neglected feet with corns and thick deformed toenails can soon prevent an old person from walking and many complications may follow the inactivity and apathy which result. Avoid tight or unduly loose footwear.

Careful hygiene, with regular washing, drying and powdering the feet, and regular attention from a chiropodist will help to prevent much disability in the elderly. "Attacks" on his own feet by an old person, or by a well-meaning friend or relative, may have disastrous long term results.

Local heat by hot water bottle or electric blanket may be very unwise where circulation to the feet is impaired. The circulating blood normally carries away local heat and spreads it throughout the body; if the heat cannot be freely dissipated the effect is to "cook" the tissues of the toes and damage may result, sometimes with severe consequences.

Bedwarming is best carried out in a more generalised way so that the body is soon warm on getting into bed.

Prevention of accidents. Falls are very common in old age, and there may be many causative factors. Not all are due to accidents, for some of the ageing changes already

[1] *See section on Insomnia.*

described may play a large part in contributing to a tendency to fall. But many falls in old age are accidental and the environment may also play an important role. We should consider:

Changes in the person
Lack of attention
Slowed responses
Impaired balance
Impaired vision
Reduced size of visual fields (i.e. area seen with both eyes open)
Muscular weakness
Legs dragging or giving away
Arthritis

and

The environment
Slippery surfaces—floors, paths, roads; especially in frosty or icy conditions
Loose or worn rugs, often on slippery surfaces
Poor light
Trailing electrical flexes
Floppy footwear, or none at all
Lack of hold—unstable furniture, no banister on staircase.

Many falls, however, cannot be attributed to accidents. Shortage of blood to certain parts of the brain may occur transiently and lead to giddiness, unsteadiness and falls. Sudden movements of the neck may bring on or aggravate this tendency, due to the anatomical disposition of some of the blood-vessels concerned, and the common occurrence of arthritis of the neck which may contribute; sometimes a movement to one particular side, or, more often, a throwing back of the head, precipitates a fall. Thus an old lady reaching up to a high shelf in her kitchen may suddenly fall to the floor; an old man looking at the fine vaulting of a church or cathedral may likewise fall to the ground. Indeed, it has been said that after 50 years of age, care should be taken to avoid all sudden neck movements. Church ceilings should be inspected by lying on a pew!

One might stress here the role of car-driving. Whip-lash injuries of the neck are increasing in incidence in car accidents, and it is quite probable that as the subject ages he will show more rapid changes in the neck which could produce the picture just described. Such an injury in a person after middle age is likely to be even more serious. The simple act of reversing a car may cause trouble if the neck is twisted too sharply or extremely; it is always important to shift one's trunk in the car seat during reversing.

Gas. Most fatalities due to gas poisoning are in people over 60. Many live alone, smell may be impaired and, most important, the old person may forget to light the gas after turning it on.

Burns and fire risks are related in that they are often due to similar situations—empty pans on lit cookers, tipping over of old oil stoves, over-stoking of coal fires, absence of adequate fire-guards, careless smoking habits, and so on.

Abuse of medicines. Old people tend to hoard bottles of medicines and tablets and often mix them indiscriminately. It is necessary to make frequent checks on just what medications are being used, and when, and to destroy all those no longer required.

In general, old people are more sensitive to drugs than are younger people, and should be given a minimum of drug treatment. Medicines should be clearly labelled with their name, use and dose, and if there is reason to believe that the patient will forget to take them correctly, one day's supply at a time should be kept in a special place and medicines should be taken only from this place. The Danes have a system of placing drugs in multi-compartment boxes, each compartment being labelled with a day of the week and relevant instructions. This system is still open to errors or abuse on the part of the patient, but is a positive contribution towards prevention of such problems and might well be used for the elderly in this country.

Insomnia. Old people seem to require less sleep than young adults, but complaints about the quality or quantity of sleep are common amongst the elderly. It is all too easy to ask for "sleeping tablets" to deal with the problem, but this may lead to more problems than it solves. There are many possible reasons for insomnia and each case requires individual consideration before rushing for the sleeping pills. Bodily discomfort may prevent or interfere with sleep; it may be due to pain (sometimes from arthritis), or to itching or to a full bladder or bowel. Frequency of passing urine may disturb sleep several times in a night.

Mental disturbances—anxiety, depression, or delirium —may also impair sleep. The pattern of sleep loss may help to pin-point the underlying cause—for instance, the anxious or confused patient may have difficulty in getting off to sleep whereas the depressed patient gets off to sleep quite well but tends to awaken in the early hours of the morning and then finds it hard to get to sleep again.

However, this pattern of insomnia is not invariable in elderly depressed patients.

The management of insomnia is primarily that of the underlying cause. Thus, pain may be relieved by pain-killing drugs and urinary and bowel problems may be amenable to treatment. Tranquillisers will help the anxious patient, and many patients with depression will respond to modern anti-depressant drugs, although the improvement may take about three weeks to appear. To tide over difficult times, sleeping drugs (hypnotics) may be used. They should not be given for long uninterrupted periods of time in the elderly, since they may lose their effectiveness and sometimes they are deleterious to the patient if continued in this way.

Certain hypnotics should be avoided in the elderly, notably the barbiturates. Barbiturates have been popular as effective hypnotics for over half a century, but the elderly tolerate them poorly, and their effects may be the opposite to those intended. Thus, restlessness and excitement may occur instead of drowsiness and sleep; some old people become very confused on barbiturates and may also lose balance and co-ordination. "Hangover" feelings are common next morning. Long-term use of barbiturates may impair mental and physical function, and yet it may be difficult to "wean" the patient from the drug.

Several alternative drugs are available as effective and safe hypnotics.

The tip of an iceberg. All the evidence points to the probability that the disabilities known to exist in the elderly of any population represents merely the tip of a large iceberg. An enormous amount of mental and physical ill-health goes unrecognised in the elderly living at home, largely because old people are often very reluctant to see their doctors or to report the appearance of some untoward sign or symptom at an early date. As a result it will be increasingly necessary to search for disability in the elderly and some sort of screening seems advisable. This might well be done by Health Visitors, attached to general practices, visiting all old people in their areas; by social workers from the local Social Services Department (Welfare Department); and by health clinics akin to infant welfare clinics, staffed by doctors and nurses. A famous pioneering clinic of this type exists at Rutherglen in Scotland, and there are others scattered over the U.K. There are also in existence many screening clinics for the detection of glaucoma and some varieties of cancer in the population as a whole. Mass X-ray facilities are also available in many areas.

Any old person who can no longer cope at home needs a *full medical assessment* by a doctor specially interested in the elderly. This inability to cope may be the only outward sign of a developing illness which, if recognised early, may be eminently treatable. In addition, all old people should be encouraged to report early any symptom which they develop as a new feature. Far too many old people are first seen by the doctor when their troubles are so far advanced that too little can be achieved with them.

Disabilities have a marked tendency to "snowball" in the elderly if left untreated. A short delay may considerably lengthen the time required for treatment and rehabilitation to be effective; a long delay may be disastrous.

In the same way, some old people place a heavy burden on the shoulders of their family and it is common to find this burden carried alone for too long by well-meaning relatives. It has been shown that there are many ways in which this burden can be shared. If carried unsupported for too long, a state of fatigue and "social sensitisation" may occur in relatives—they become allergic, as it were, to their elderly relative, and may then wish to be rid of the burden of care by having her sent into, say, a hospital in the hope that she will never be sent home again. If help is provided by the community at an earlier stage, the overall sharing of the burden usually leads to a greater ability on the part of the family to cope and a far more humane and practicable solution results.

The moral is that help for the elderly, when required, should be sought early: all burdens may then be minimised, breakdown of the situation avoided or at least postponed for a long time; and all agencies involved—including relatives—will feel better motivated to continuing to play their part at the appropriate times.

Attitudes to older people

"Every man desires to live long, but no man would be old."—Swift.

This pessimistic view of old age has been shared by many people from very early times, exemplified in the 12th Chapter of Ecclesiastes and by Shakespeare (*As You Like It*, Act II):

> ". . . last scene of all
> That ends this strange eventful history
> Is second childishness and mere oblivion,
> Sans teeth, sans eyes, sans taste, sans everything".

Accordingly, attempts at rejuvenation have been made for thousands of years—but unsuccessfully.

Yet *healthy* old age can be a most satisfying period of life, a time when pressures due to ambition and the "rat race" have eased, tranquillity may be enjoyed, achievements looked upon with satisfaction, and when many may profit by the wisdom and judgment accumulated over the years. There is time to think, and time to do many things formerly denied by time or other commitments.

This more positive attitude to old age has, fortunately, become more common over the last quarter of a century, and the aim of all those actively concerned with the elderly must be to maintain old people's physical and mental activity and health and so enable them to obtain the most from their later years. After all, a lady of 60 may live to be 90, and 30 years is a long time! How fruitless and negative to be pessimistic about such a long period of one's life—no less than one-third of the whole lifespan of that individual. One only has to think of how much may be accomplished between birth and 30 years, or even between 20 and 50 years, to realise that *the potential inherent in these later years is very great indeed*, and every attempt should be made to realise it.

This example shows how important it is to adopt a positive and optimistic approach, so that those possible 30 years of old age are meaningful and full of their own satisfaction and achievements. This is what we mean by "adding life to years", which is a major aim of those working to help the elderly.

Of course, many people do not remain in good health throughout their later life, and the quality of their lives may be the less for that reason. But in these days it is possible to do much to help to prevent disability in the elderly, and to help to improve their health if they do fall ill. And by health we include functional ability to cope with their daily lives as independently as possible.

Many people—old and young—have little or no idea of just how much can be done in this direction, and still cling to outmoded pessimistic attitudes. Much education, both public and professional, is needed to emphasise how justified is an optimistic approach towards old people, even when they fall ill, and how to marshal appropriate help at the earliest possible time.

It is all too easy to attribute a falling-off in health or abilities to "just old age" when proper assessment may reveal some easily remediable situation, correction of which might make enormous differences to the physical and mental well-being of that individual, either immediately or at some future time. The term "old age" then becomes a convenient sort of "dustbin" into which awkward or annoying symptoms or personal failures may be swept; but the price to be paid for this carelessness may prove to be very high indeed.

What matters most, then, is to identify such difficulties *early* and obtain skilled assessment of their significance and proper management. Thus, when an old lady, living alone, becomes unable to manage entirely unaided *for the first time*, a medical assessment may be wise. So the first time she requests home help or meals on wheels, or is noted to need them, she should be seen by a doctor interested in old people, for this may be how an illness may make its first outward appearance.

Let us consider further some of the attitudes met with in individuals, in the relatives and friends of old people, and in the wider community.

(*a*) *Individuals.* Much depends on the personality and the emotional make-up of the person concerned—it has been said that a person's general adjustment to ageing is profoundly affected by his feeling about age.

The outgoing, cheerful personality will adopt a positive attitude. He will look forward to his eventual retirement in a constructive way, and will plan the various activities he will undertake—things he has enjoyed doing in earlier life, but which he has had all too little time for; things he has always wanted to do but for which he has never been able to find time; people and places to visit; enjoyment of his family; and so on. If he becomes ill or disabled, he will be a " trier", co-operating with his medical and nursing advisers and other helpers, and showing drive, initiative and energy in his attempt to aid his recovery.

But people are not always cast in this mould—indeed, only a minority are—and various other types of personality will predispose to different approaches to ageing and disability. Some individuals are unduly passive and over-accepting of their problems, and these will make little positive effort towards the full life in old age, especially if they fall ill. Others are weak personalities, who are easily depressed and over-anxious; blows of fate are seen as catastrophes or even as "punishment" and these people will also fail to achieve a full and active old age. They are difficult to manage if they become disabled, and are often hypochondriacal whether physically ill or not. They often regard old age as a time to "rest" and this desire for inactivity may be hard to overcome, to their own detriment.

A few personalities are more difficult still—some suspicious and some unpredictable.

Morale has been defined as a state of psychological well-being derived from a sense of purpose and usefulness and confidence. It is likely to be highest in old people living an independent existence at home.

Studies have found morale to be less when some independence had been forfeited, as in some types of residential accommodation such as grouped dwellings for the elderly; and morale was lowest in long-stay hospital patients who had given up their independence altogether.

Emotional factors are important in the sick and disabled especially those with prolonged disabilities confined to long-stay hospital wards. The world of such patients shrinks and events take on a different significance for them. The patient becomes more childish and petulant, selfish and demanding, intolerant and hypochondriacal. Later, outbursts of difficult behaviour may alternate with apathy, producing the picture known as institutional neurosis.

It is clear that the personality of the patient has suffered gravely in these circumstances. Yet the integrity of the personality is of fundamental importance in the well-being of old people. Marjorie Fry[1] expressed it thus: "To the administrator an individual may be just 'that old woman—I think her name is Jones', but to herself she is the Katie Jones who won a prize for scripture and had the smallest waist in the class—with a thousand other distinctive features—who just happens to be old." The importance of personality has been emphasised in the section of this book dealing with incontinence of urine.

Hospitalisation (an ugly word which has come to stay) is an attack on the personality of an old person. Prolonged hospitalisation is likely to destroy that personality.

For these reasons every effort must be made to keep old people's stay in hospital as short as possible, and to avoid long-stay admissions in every possible case by every means available. Most old people, even those with considerable disability, wish to live at home, and all who devote their energies to the health and well-being of the elderly are agreed that home is the best place for them in most instances.

(b) *Relatives and friends.* In maintaining health and preventing disability in old people, relatives and friends

1 Fry, M. (1955), *Old Age in the Modern World*. Edinburgh and London, Livingstone.

are often involved. Their task is greater when the old person is less than fully independent or—as in many cases —far from independent. The attitude of relatives and friends towards old age and the elderly will play a large part in their satisfactions and frustrations.

Much depends on whether the old person lives alone and is visited by relatives and friends, or whether she lives *with* relatives or friends. There are often problems in a domestic situation where elderly relatives reside with younger generations. Personality problems often arise, as much due to the old person's forgetfulness and tendency to repetition, as to more intrusive difficulties like interference in household or parent-child affairs or a tendency to selfish or anti-social behaviour. Apart from these matters, the physical limitations of the available accommodation may add to the difficulties, possibly by throwing the generations together more than they would wish. The three-bedroom three-up and one- or two-down arrangement does not cater satisfactorily for the three-generation household. Grandchildren may irritate the old person, and the old person may irritate her own son or daughter, if not the grandchildren as well.

Of prime importance in such a situation is the ability of the younger people to disengage themselves from irritating situations. Old people resist change and their personalities have narrowed and hardened. They are not going to change their ideas and ways now. Their children and grandchildren, however, are young enough to retain flexibility in their behaviour patterns and it is up to them not to jump to the bait, so to speak, each time they feel provoked by their elderly relative. They must make allowances for the rigidity, the memory-losses, and the occasional lack of judgment and tact in the elderly, and so *they must not react to old people as they would to*

65

young people doing or saying the same thing. Only by thus disengaging themselves from such situations can they preserve sufficient calm in the household.

Successful multi-generation households may be seen to be adopting this policy—although in some, of course, the older person fits in far more easily than in others, so that peace-threatening situations do not then arise with any great frequency.

Over-protectiveness. Many relatives and friends adopt an over-protective attitude towards the elderly. This can be harmful and lead to loss of initiative and excessive immobility in the old person, particularly dangerous if it leads to long periods spent in bed.

This attitude is usually well-meant—it is often thought that plenty of rest is beneficial to the elderly, and there may be real risks in allowing frail old people to move about the house freely. The main risk is usually the risk of falling. But, as stated earlier, old people do not need an undue amount of rest, and spending long hours in bed is as harmful as it is unnecessary. Furthermore, the whole of life involves some risks, and the prevention of falls by inducing immobility is totally wrong—far better to provide walking aids and walking practice for such persons—with help from the hospital geriatric department if necessary. After all, improved walking efficiency means that falls are less likely. In some instances, immobility is encouraged by relatives who have to go out for a while, or who are away overnight, by the use of sedatives and sleeping tablets. This is a risky procedure, unless carefully supervised; although adequate night sedation may well be necessary, injudicious use of sedative drugs during the day may be very harmful. Expert advice will be needed in such cases, and a doctor should always control this aspect of management of the elderly.

It is especially important that relatives who accept such medical advice, which may lead to calculated risks, should not feel guilty about so doing. They should lean on the knowledge that they have taken expert advice and can reasonably do no more. Tensions and stresses within families are often considerable enough without being increased unnecessarily.

Importance of early warning. Many relatives and friends call for help too late, and then demand rapid action—"something must be done, doctor". In such instances, it may be difficult to provide adequate help at short notice, or to get rapid admission to a hospital or residential home.

The overburdened relatives may then blame the National Health Service, pointing out that they—or the patient—have paid their contributions for years, etc. This righteous statement, however, although factually accurate, rarely helps. Here the problem has been the wrong attitude about calling for help at an early enough stage to prevent breakdowns in the home management from developing. Forward planning, on the other hand, can save many a crisis, and preserve the health and happiness of the patient and his relatives.

Once the patient is in hospital there is in some instances a feeling on the part of the relatives or friends that she should remain there for a long time, or even for the rest of her life. This is an old-fashioned attitude, harking back to the "bad old days" of custodial care, prior to the introduction of the National Health Services, when old people were often not thought of as being candidates for active treatment and rehabilitation and return to the community.

Old ideas die hard; but they must be thrown overboard, for the modern hospital geriatric department assesses each patient fully and wherever possible plans a programme for the patient which is aimed at returning him or her to the community at the earliest time compatible with her disability (see preceding paragraph). One reason for the persistence of the old idea is the persistence of old buildings: one-time workhouses often house geriatric departments working full-out in the modern manner with active treatment and rehabilitation. It is perhaps hard to envisage modern medicine being carried out in some of these far-from-modern buildings but appearances are deceptive, and the facts are well worth finding out.

Any intelligent relative responsible for an old person would do well to visit the local geriatric department to find out just how it operates and just how much help it can, in fact, provide. (See Chapter 2.)

Guilt. There is no doubt that many relatives feel guilty if they cannot provide total care for their elderly relation, or if they fail to eliminate all risks to the old person.

This feeling of guilt is usually undeserved but may be difficult to overcome. It can, unfortunately, lead to difficulties with the very people and departments who are doing their best to help the old person, for it is often converted into criticisms and complaints based on emotions and superficial impressions rather than full knowledge of the medical aspects of the case, and of the principles of modern geriatric medicine. Such relatives are usually helped by an informal talk with their general practitioner, the consultant physician in the geriatric department or—if the patient is at home or in a residential home—with a social worker from the local authority Social Services Department.

(c) *The community.* "Dishonour not the old; we shall all be numbered among them."—*The Apocrypha.* Community attitudes to old people have always been important, but have varied widely according to the type and situation of the community and the disabilities of the old people.

Classical writers emphasised the care of the aged. Primitive communities, where relatively few persons reach old age, revere their old people for their wisdom as well as their scarcity value. Multigeneration households are common, and the elderly continue to have a role in society until very late in their lives or even into after-life as in China.

In Western civilisations, however, there has been marked ageing of the populations as a whole, with many more people reaching old age, as described in Chapter I. Furthermore, in our society today there has been a de-valuation of old age and a great emphasis on youth. In these days of emphasis on productivity and material values, the elderly have generally lost significance in the community—and they feel it, which must be a contributory factor in some of their problems. Patterns of housing, work and the dispersal of families have contributed to the picture, so that now the elderly constitute a "problem" all too often—either individually or as a group.

Many years ago, our society rejected the sick and the old and frail, and the practice was to put them "out of sight and out of mind". They were often regarded in none too kindly a manner by society as a whole, though devotedly cared for by their nurses.

Later, this rejection by society largely gave way to

charitable acceptance, but even then the element of charity brought its problems and the "acceptance" was often passive.

Now society is more prepared to be actively involved in rehabilitating the elderly and the ill, and yet certain faulty attitudes persist from former times. Thus, stigma still attaches to certain types of illness, and certain types of hospitals. Many hospitals in this country are old, yet excellent modern medicine is practised within them. Many geriatric hospitals are still in former workhouses (Public Assistance Institutions) and the old people of today can remember earlier conditions in, and stories about, those institutions in their "workhouse" days. There is then a reluctance to enter such a hospital for treatment, based on an ignorance or lack of appreciation of how they have changed. The idea that modern techniques of treatment and rehabilitation may take place in such buildings does not always find acceptance by the community.

Other factors may contribute to the reluctance of an old person to enter hospital—lack of trust of doctors, friends or relatives combined with a suspicion that the patient is being "put away" and will lose her home, her independence, freedom and personality. Such fears and mistrust may be allayed by gentle reassurance and explanation from the general practitioner and perhaps a social worker. There may be a relative or friend who has been in the hospital previously, as a patient or a visitor, who can offer her experience as reassurance for the patient. Hospital "open days" also help to inform and reassure the community about modern methods of treatment and rehabilitation.

Yet once a patient has been well-cared-for in a geriatric hospital the initial resistance to admission there may be replaced by an equal or even greater resistance to discharge home! The old idea of "custodial care" dies hard in the public mind, and this is not confined to relatives and friends but may sometimes be seen in neighbours, clergymen, social workers, and nurses and doctors too.

Only continuing education of the public as a whole can overcome these outmoded ideas. Everyone concerned with the elderly should realise the full value of rehabilitation and the desirability of spending one's later years at home whenever possible.

Retirement

The age of retirement for men is 65 years and for women 60 years, and from these ages men and women respectively are normally entitled to receive a weekly retirement pension. These are arbitrary ages, administratively convenient, but not always "right" for the individual. Many men are working very effectively at 65 years of age, and their experience will often be extensive, so that their compulsory retirement at that age might well seem illogical. For those whose "life is their work" there may follow a period of frustration and enforced idleness which impairs their health. It is sobering to remember once again that that period can be as long as 30 years!

Undue dependence on work is not good for any man, and outside interests throughout life make that life more complete; such interests are essential in those about to retire. The housewife does not retire, of course, but the sharp transition from organised work to retirement is a problem for many men—a problem of time, activity and finance. For these reasons, retirement must be prepared for well ahead of its time of arrival.

Pre-retirement courses. More and more pre-retirement

71

courses are being organised, by local education authorities or by large business concerns. Employees may be released for, say, one day per week to attend these courses, which consist of talks and discussions on finances, health, occupation, hobbies, housing, and welfare services. In some areas there are local pre-retirement associations or retirement councils. Their organisation is supported and encouraged by the central Pre-Retirement Association (this, and other addresses are given at the end of Part I of this book). This Association, from whom information may be obtained, publishes several useful books concerning retirement and its problems, and can recommend other relevant literature.

The Industrial Society is a voluntary body promoting the best use of human resources in industry, commerce and the public services. It has close links with the Pre-Retirement Association, with which it has recently formed an Older Worker Advisory Panel; on this Panel are represented several firms and organisations particularly concerned with the older worker. Its aims include retraining in middle age, training for retirement and part-time work after retirement.

Retirement and health. "The rhubarb that no one picks goes to seed."—Wilder Penfield.

Although retirement in itself has no particular effect on health, it may produce discontent and frustration leading to apathy and a very real breakdown in mental and physical health. An important factor in this situation is the pre-retirement attitude of the individual. Without some forethought, and preferably instruction, in the years before retirement, the retired person may find himself bored, lonely, unhappy and in financial difficulties.

It is, in fact, not uncommon to discover men whose

lives seemed to "fold up" upon retirement. With the sudden leisure and lack of the stimulation provided by work a man may simply give up his interest in life and this is why ill-health in old age is often attributed to compulsory retirement.

Work during retirement. Apart from the mental activity provided by hobbies, old and new, working during retirement may be of great value to many. This work may be voluntary or paid; a paid job will usually be part-time, since beyond a certain income (at present £9.50 per week per pensioner) deductions are made from the retirement pension of persons aged 65–70; and few will want full-time employment after 70, when the earnings rule is waived.

Special employment agencies may be found in different areas, set up by voluntary bodies or even private individuals or groups, or sometimes by the local Retirement Council.

Advice may be sought from the local Old People's Welfare Council; the Council of Social Service; the Citizens' Advice Bureau; or by contacting one of the national bodies (see pages 74/75.

Some firms give out work to be done at home, but careful enquiry should be made before becoming involved in such an arrangement to determine the precise conditions and rewards.

Sheltered workshops exist in a few areas. A pioneer one was set up in Finsbury by Dr. Blyth-Brooke, and some industrial firms have followed suit, especially for their own employees. Dr. Snellgrove of Luton has made valuable contributions to employment of the elderly and has written a book about it.[1]

[1] D. R. Snellgrove (1965), *Elderly Employed.* Luton: White Crescent Press Ltd.

In Glasgow the Retirement Council has encouraged the Foundation of Retired Employees' Associations formed by workers retiring from a firm who then remain in the ken of the personnel and welfare officer. These associations hold meetings in the firms' premises, newsletters are sent out, and each member is given pre-paid postcards to send to the personnel officer if he is in need of help. A sender of such a card will be visited and in this way an old person need not feel isolated. There are also visiting committees to call on the sick at home or in hospital. There are at least ten such groups in Glasgow and the movement is developing and could well be copied elsewhere.

The Birmingham Retirement Council has formed a number of groups for studying various subjects and providing social contacts, and these are very successful. The groups are known as FIR-Cone (Friends-In-Retirement) Groups and now number over fifty. Each group has a special interest or hobby and seeks an instructor with experience in the subject from within its own ranks; failing this, the help of the local education authority is sought.

Some useful addresses

Age Concern (formerly National Old People's Welfare Council)
55 Gower Street, London WC1E 6HJ.

Civil Service Retirement Fellowship
230 Abbey House, Victoria Street, London, SW1.

Employment Fellowship
Drayton House, Gordon Street, London, WC1.

Scottish Old People's Welfare Committee
18 Claremont Crescent, Edinburgh EH7 4HX.

National Council for the Elderly in Wales
2 Cathedral Road, Cardiff.

Pre-Retirement Association
35 Queen Anne Street, London W1M 9FB.

The Industrial Society
Robert Hyde House, 48 Bryanston Square, London W1H
    8AH.

A Practical Guide to Help Available

In the community

THERE is a wide variety of services available to the elderly
living at home, but the precise details and strengths and
weaknesses of these services vary from one part of the
country to another. A brief description of these services
is given here, followed by practical advice about how to
mobilise them. Although it might seem logical if all these
services came under one administrative channel, this is
unfortunately not the case. The general organisation of
the services is shown in Fig. 2 and discussed further in
Chapter 6. Note that reorganisation of the National
Health Service is scheduled for 1974.

The "Social Services Department" has replaced the
former "Welfare Department" and is taking over the full
range of personal social services under the reorganisation
recommended by the Seebohm Report (see Appendix 1).

Since at least 95 per cent of the old people in this
country are living in the community, it follows that the
brunt of medical care for the elderly falls upon the family
doctor, or general practitioner. The G.P. is the keystone
of our Health Service, and he is in the best position to
help and advise in matters of medical and social care
concerning old people. He will have a broad knowledge of
the services and facilities available and how to call upon

FIG. 2.   ORGANISATION OF HEALTH AND SOCIAL SERVICES

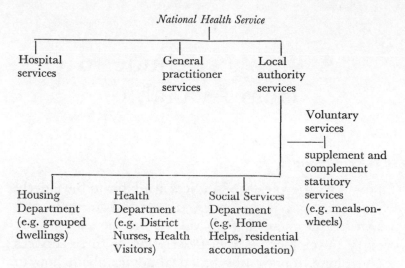

National Health Service

Hospital services — General practitioner services — Local authority services

Voluntary services — supplement and complement statutory services (e.g. meals-on-wheels)

Housing Department (e.g. grouped dwellings) — Health Department (e.g. District Nurses, Health Visitors) — Social Services Department (e.g. Home Helps, residential accommodation)

them; but even he cannot be expected to know every possible line of approach since these are now so many and diverse, as the ensuing sections will show.

These try to keep old people functioning adequately in their own homes, and are therefore known as "domiciliary services" or, more colloquially, "social props"— they help to "prop up" or support a person so that he or she may lead a basically independent existence at home.

If they fail to achieve this end, then the local authority has the task of providing residential accommodation for the elderly—the "in" term for Old People's Homes, about which more will be said later.

Recent legislation has placed local authority personal services in the charge of the Director of Social Services for the county or borough. Medically-related services are organised by the Health Department of the county, city, or borough, except that mental health services are now included in the Social Services Department.

1. *Home helps.* The Home Help will keep the house clean, do the shopping and the washing and perhaps cook a meal. She is not expected to undertake nursing duties. She attends for a period of time in the day which varies according to need and availability and may even call twice in the same day. She may attend on all or only some weekdays, but the service is rarely available at weekends. In some areas, however—mainly urban—weekend service may be available.

There is a charge for Home Help Service which depends on the recipient's income and on the cost of private domestic help in the area concerned. Each recipient is assessed and an appropriate charge is made; those on Supplementary Benefits will be assessed at a minimum rate and this amount will be provided by the Supplementary Benefits Office. No one should therefore feel that she cannot afford Home Help.

Sometimes a "good neighbours" scheme is available —a neighbour offers help and may then be paid by the local authority. Similarly a relative who regularly helps an old person in this way may be eligible for payment as a Home Help.

The availability of Home Helps varies from one part of the country to another. An adequate service probably requires that there should be at least ten Home Helps per thousand elderly people in the community. This is the figure found in Warrington (Lancs.), for example, and exceeded in Hackney (London) which has fourteen Home Helps per thousand elderly. Contrast Bournemouth, which has less than one per thousand old persons and Brent (London) which has only three per thousand old persons. The national average in England and Wales was five per thousand elderly in 1965. Recruitment of Home Helps is affected by competition from local industries or other domestic opportunities.

To obtain the best results the Home Help and the relatives or neighbours should plan together how to allocate their efforts.

One problem which arises occasionally is an old person's refusal to accept Home Help—for various reasons, such as intrusion on privacy, lack of trust, dislike of an individual Home Help's personality or habits, or financial stringency. Whilst these objections may be soundly based in some cases, all too often they are more in the nature of excuses, part of a general tendency of some old people to resist accepting outside help.

Much time and effort may need to be spent in persuading such an old person to change her mind; sometimes it takes a breakdown in health or admission to hospital to make her realise that she must now accept the need for assistance with domestic chores and shopping. However, it should be emphasised that if an old lady can cope with her housework and does not really need a Home Help, it is far better to avoid pressurising her to accept one, since independence—provided it is real and not imagined—is one of the most valuable assets an old person can have. It is to be encouraged in every possible way. The acid test is the success of her unaided efforts.

A secondary advantage of the Home Help Service is the human contact it provides; some old people have few social contacts, and the Home Help's visit may be a potent force in the prevention of isolation and loneliness in such cases.

2. *Meals-on-wheels.* This important service provides hot meals which are prepared in central kitchens in vari-

ous areas and distributed by car or van to old people in their own homes.

In many instances this service is actually run by voluntary organisations, usually the Women's Royal Voluntary Service, but with financial aid from the local authority. In some areas the local authority itself runs the service directly.

It is rare for meals-on-wheels to be provided daily. They are, of course, meant for housebound persons who cannot cook for themselves or go out to lunch clubs, day centres or relatives. The demand usually exceeds the supply so that the meals may only be sent in to an old person two or three times a week. In some areas, however, those who need them may receive these meals every day, even including weekends. A small charge is made for these meals—rarely more than 10p (they are subsidised by the local authority). Only about 1 per cent of old people in the U.K. receive meals-on-wheels, but there is reason to believe that many more would like them.

Regrettably, old people tend to waste the meals sent in to them, either by leaving them or by throwing them away or giving them to a pet animal. It is not uncommon to find an isolated old person whose cat looks as healthy and well-fed as its owner looks ill and undernourished. Some old people refuse to accept meals-on-wheels on some pretext or another. Each unsatisfactory situation of this sort needs individual handling by those coming into contact with the old person.

The provision of meals-on-wheels to an old person does not imply that they will be delivered indefinitely. Periodic reviews of the need for the meals, and their value to the recipient, should be made by those concerned with the original prescription of meals for that person, and the frequency of the supply of meals may be altered accordingly, or the service discontinued where no longer needed. In practice, however, once the meals are started they are often continued indefinitely. They are certainly not withdrawn without adequate reason.

The value of the brief contact with the outside world is a secondary but real advantage of receiving meals-on-wheels.

3. *Home nursing.* District Nurses do superb work in patients' homes, and in the case of old people this often means very difficult home surroundings. They call to give injections, dress ulcers or skin disease, bandage varicose veins, give enemas and help with washing, bathing, dressing and undressing of patients. Male district nurses are especially helpful in caring for heavy patients and certain male patients—including those needing catheter changes at regular intervals. District nurses provide an important liaison between the local authority health department and family and hospital doctors.

This service—which is free—cannot provide continuous nursing, and may be overloaded if the problems of the elderly patient become too great. The District Nurse calls once or twice a day if necessary; if the nursing needs cannot be met by these visits the patient requires to be treated in hospital—in the interests of all concerned.

District nurses are often attached to specific general practices and there is an early and encouraging trend towards secondment of district nurses to hospital geriatric departments on a part-time or full-time basis, so that continuity of care and fullest possible exchange of information can be achieved. The preventive value of such an arrangement will be obvious.

Some areas employ Nursing Auxiliaries who will give

baths, cut toenails and wash hair. They may be known as bathing attendants. This service relieves pressure on district nurses. Again, in certain areas local authorities may arrange for a minibus or other form of transport to take old people to public baths or, where there is no hot water in an old person's home, large vacuum flasks of hot water may be delivered.

4. *Health visitors.* These are nurses who undergo further training to equip them to play a primarily preventive role in medical and nursing care of patients, young and old. Their work is familiar to many mothers, because of their role in ante-natal and post-natal care and infant and child welfare. They have played a large part in helping to keep tuberculosis under control. They also have a large part to play in the well-being of the elderly. Like District Nurses, they are often attached to general practices and some may be seconded to geriatric departments.

The Health Visitor has much to offer old people and their relatives and friends, in endeavouring to promote "positive health" and to prevent disease and disability. This role in health education is very important. She may also detect trouble at an early stage, before it becomes apparent to the patient or his untrained well-wishers; and she can sometimes persuade a difficult or stubborn old person to accept medical assistance or "social props". She can thus help to uncover the submerged part of the "iceberg" of disease and disability in the elderly. It is well-known that old people suffer from much more ill-health than is known to their family doctors, since elderly persons are often unwilling to report any untoward symptoms and resent "outside interference".

They frequently attribute any difficulties to "old age"

and in this way their problems may ultimately become magnified. The Health Visitor has a major part to play in tackling such problems and she is likely to be—with the general practice to which she is attached—the cornerstone of preventive geriatrics in the future.

5. *Preventive care clinics.* A few local authorities have set up Consultative Health Centres for old people, with a view to prevention and early detection of disease and disability in the elderly. Opportunity is also taken for health education.

In addition, screening clinics exist for the detection of such conditions at glaucoma, diabetes and cancer; these clinics are not, of course, confined to the elderly.

6. *Night watching service.* This is all too rarely available, but in some parts of the country a night-sitter can be sent to an old person's home to help tide over a particular illness or in the last days of life; or sometimes to give relatives a well-deserved break. The night-sitter is not a nurse and cannot do more than a relative might; but this service may prevent the need for hospital admission.

7. *Laundry service.* Some local authority health departments provide a free laundry service for incontinent patients at home. Wet sheets are placed in special plastic bags provided, and these are picked up regularly by van and clean sheets left in their place. Clothing may also be included in this service, which is invaluable for helping to keep old people at home, and could with advantage be extended to more areas of the country.

Incontinence pads may be provided but their disposal is not easy. A collection-service is organised for these in some areas, as for wet sheets. For other items which may be provided for incontinent patients see next Section (8).

8. *Equipment loans.* A wide variety of equipment for medical and nursing purposes can be supplied on loan by the local authority, including walking frames, bedcradles, backrests. To help with toilet problems, bedpans, urinals, commodes, plastic or mackintosh sheeting, incontinence pads, urinal appliances for men and incontinence pants for women are available. New bedding can be subsidised or bought if the need is demonstrated. Even beds, with any necessary attachments such as a hand-grip on a pole ("monkey grip"), can be provided, and in these cases the appropriate height of the bed can be tailored to the needs of each individual patient. Similar considerations apply to armchairs, which may have a special ejector mechanism to lift the subject gently from a sitting to a standing position—useful in some cases of arthritis of the hips, for example. Hydraulic or electric hoists may be supplied where necessary to help an old person in and out of bed or bath or car.

The general rule about the source of such equipment is that local authorities supply mainly nursing equipment, whereas hospitals supply 'tailor-made" appliances, or equipment specifically needed to enable a discharge from hospital to be effected. This may include the loan of a wheelchair; for more permanent use the patient may have a wheelchair ordered specially for him by a Consultant Physician; it is supplied via the hospital, by a local Ministry of Pensions depot.

Wheelchairs may be lightweight and folding for ease of transport, or may be more solid; one or both side-pieces —attached to the arms of the chair—may be removable

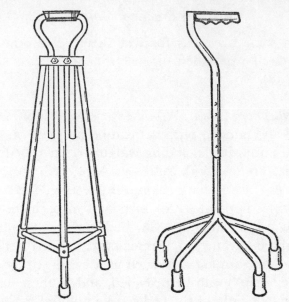

Walking aids: tripod and quadruped.

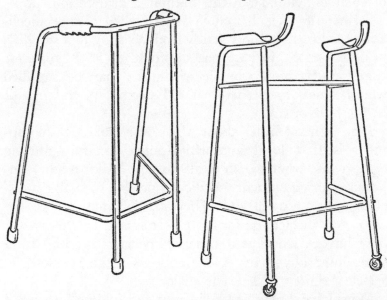

Walking frame: standard
model.

Walking frame with gutters for
arms, and handgrips, useful
for patients with arthritis of
wrists and hands.

Note wheels at front only, for
ease of progression without risk
of runaway accidents.

to allow the patient to transfer himself sideways to bed or commode or W.C. A board may be needed between wheelchair and bed to allow the patient to slide between the two. These and other aspects of life in a wheelchair are taught to patients whenever necessary by the occupational therapist, whose primary objective is to restore, maintain and develop function in people with disabilities. She will also consider what other equipment, gadgets and home modifications might be advisable to make life easier for patients returning home (see Chapter 7).

In some cases, voluntary organisations such as the British Red Cross Society will lend equipment, including wheelchairs. Other equipment available includes gadgets designed to act as aids to daily living (also see Chapter 7).

9. *Home adaptations.* Apart from improving the patient as far as possible, it is sometimes possible to improve her environment too, by making adaptations to her home—ramps instead of steps, handrails around W.C.'s or on staircases, wider doors, raising electric sockets and so on. Simple details like a change of height of W.C. seat may make a big difference to personal independence. A gas cooker with safety-devices can be bought or rented, and the cost can be recovered from the Supplementary Pensions Office if the old person receives a Supplementary Pension.

10. *Chiropody.* There are various arrangements for chiropody, in local authority clinics or day centres, at home or at the chiropodist's surgery, and in hospitals and geriatric day hospitals.

11. *Recuperative holidays.* These may be provided by

the local authority on the family doctor's recommendation, or by voluntary bodies.

12. *Library services*. Mobile library services, including large-print books, are available in many areas. For the blind, books in braille or Moon type may be had on loan; Moon is better suited for the elderly blind person, being based on normal type, easy to learn, and needing less sensitivity in the fingers which read it. Social Services departments may pay for the loan of a playback machine for talking books. These books are recorded on tape cassettes playing up to thirteen hours each. Tapes are lent free and may, like all reading materials for the blind, be sent post-free.

13. *Social Workers*. The local authority Social Services Department employs social workers to establish and maintain contact with old people who appear to be failing to cope at home. They can arrange for the provision of the various "social props" mentioned above and they also assess their clients if the question of residential accommodation arises. They establish liaison between the Social Services Department and the family doctor and hospital services, and may join in case conferences within the geriatric department when considering the overall welfare of patients attending there—in the day hospital or in the wards, for example.

The Mental Health Social Worker has corresponding functions and tries to maintain old people with mild mental disturbances in the community. This is the intention of the Mental Health Act (1958) which aims to prevent unnecessary admissions to mental hospitals. There are many aspects to this subject which cannot be discussed in detail here—so much depends on the type of case and the home circumstances. Should home management fail, the doctor will inform the Mental Health Social Worker who will assist in arranging transfer of the patient to an appropriate hospital. There is always a Mental Health Social Worker on duty to cope with emergencies by day and by night.

14. *Services for the blind.* Lack of sight which makes it impossible "to perform any work for which eyesight is essential" qualifies a person for entry to the register of blind persons which is kept by the local authority. It will be realised that blindness need not be complete for inclusion on the blind register. There are several advantages to being on this register, and some may be shared by the partially-sighted who are not eligible for registration.

Visits by Social Workers ensure that the blind or partially blind person is made aware of the various financial concessions, aids, clubs, handicraft classes, and rehabilitation arrangements available for the blind. Special holidays are also available.

Reading materials and talking books have been considered under Library Services—see Section 12.

15. *Services for the deaf.* Local authorities provide services for the totally deaf and the partially deaf—in some cases through a local voluntary organisation for the deaf. Social workers visit and help, much as in the case of the blind. Advice is given about hearing aids, finger-spelling and lip-reading, and the problems of deafness in the elderly are discussed with relatives. Gadgets such as a flashing light to indicate ringing of doorbells or alarm clocks are supplied.

16. *The physically handicapped.* Disabled old people may become registered as handicapped and participate in facilities provided by the local authority for the handicapped of all ages. Many old people, however, take part in these facilities whether so registered or not.

17. *Day centres.* Many local authorities run day centres, some of which may be specially equipped for the disabled, others geared to the elderly in general, and yet others providing especially for the mentally ill and handicapped. These centres are primarily social and diversional in function, but may include facilities for chiropody or hairdressing.

A subsidised lunch and hot drinks are available. Old people attending these centres usually spend a morning and afternoon there at least once a week. Transport is provided if required, but is often insufficient to meet the needs of everyone eligible, and may become a bottleneck which causes a long delay before attendances can begin.

Day Centres should be distinguished from Day Hospitals, which are considered later.

18. *Occupational therapy and physiotherapy.* In a few areas some occupational therapy can be provided at home, and, more rarely, physiotherapy. Travelling is often wasteful of the time of these highly-trained therapists, and it seems unlikely that these services will expand much on a domiciliary basis.

19. *Financial need.* Radios may be borrowed for indefinite periods by old people, from the Wireless for the Bedridden Society (20 Wimpole Street, London W.1), via the local Social Services department. The applicant need not be bedridden but must show financial need.

Television sets are less freely available but may be provided; or the licence fee may be paid if the patient owns her own set.

Telephone charges may be met by an addition to the supplementary pension if the recipient is housebound, living alone, and is isolated.

Under the recent Chronically Sick and Disabled Persons Act 1970, (see p. 97) local authorities are encouraged to provide or help provide TV and telephone for the severely handicapped and if necessary, special equipment to help the handicapped in using the telephone or TV set.

20. *Residential accommodation.* The local authority Social Services Department is required to provide residential accommodation for old people and others who have no home of their own or who are in need of care and attention. This requirement is laid down in Part III of the National Assistance Act (1948) and the residential homes provided are often referred to as "Part Three" accommodation.

Most places in these homes are taken by elderly people whose average age is about 80 years, and who often have a considerable degree of frailty or even some frank physical and/or mental disability. Indeed, the borderline between those fit enough to be cared for in a residential home and those needing hospital treatment may be blurred, and there is always a middle band of frail semi-dependent old people who seem to fall between the two and who may indeed oscillate between residential homes and hospitals.

Over the years this problem has increased; the homes which once required virtually full fitness and independence in their applicants for residence have now had to face the fact that the majority of such applicants are in need of some degree of personal care. Although incontinence of urine has usually been a bar to acceptance in residential accommodation, even this is now accepted—if not too severe—in some homes. Incontinence is, however, more likely to be tolerated if it develops in a person already resident in the home, rather than if present at the time of a new entry. Of course, it requires appropriate investigation and management and may only be transient.

The decision as to acceptability for a residential home is made by Social Workers from the Social Services Department; although doctors, in hospital or outside it, may make recommendations in the case of individual patients, *the final word rests with the Social Services Department.* This point is not well understood by the public, who often expect the family doctor or hospital doctor (especially, perhaps in a geriatric department) to be able to place an old person directly in a residential home. This cannot be done, although one might feel it to be a matter of regret.

There is tremendous variation in the type and quality of residential homes, and also in their number and distribution. In recent years, there has been a progressive abolition—and demolition—of the large, bleak old public assistance institution buildings sometimes used as residential homes, and these have given way to smaller purpose-built homes for thirty to fifty residents. The new homes are furnished and equipped to a high standard, and are usually centrally-heated.

Some local authorities have special homes for the mentally frail; others include such residents in their ordinary residential homes. Much depends on staffing and, here again, there are many variations. Some homes employ trained nurses and some do not.

Eligibility for residential care in a particular area depends on residential qualifications. It is easier for an old person to get into a home in the area in which she has been living than in another area altogether. There is something to be said for considering the future possibility of requiring such accommodation *well ahead of the likely time of need*; it is a simple matter to leave one's name on the waiting list and to decline the vacancy if there is no need for the move when one's name comes up. The alternative of discovering a sudden urgent need is much less desirable and can rarely be acted upon; the waiting period may then be most uncomfortable and even risky—and intolerable to distressed relatives or neighbours.

No old person is offered a place in residential accommodation unless he or she wishes it and signs a form of agreement. Thus no one can be placed in a residential home against her will—except in rare instances where an old person is a public health hazard—to herself and to the community.

Several difficulties inevitably result from this role: some old people who are failing to cope alone at home would clearly thrive in the shelter of residential accommodation, but many refuse to consider such a move. There are many reasons for this attitude: love of one's own home, often of over half a century's duration; a fierce sense of independence, even flying in the face of reality; and fears connected with the old peoples' home. It is a "going away", and there is often the fear of loss of rights, freedom and independence. Such fears are groundless but may be hard or impossible to overcome. There may also be a feeling of stigma—a hangover from former days of institutions and workhouses.

Such fears may lead to, or stem from, mistrust of relatives, friends and professional advisers who are trying very genuinely to help and give good advice. Since these parties are usually those who will bear the burden if residential care is refused, the situation is often difficult for all concerned. Social workers, with their training in psychology and interview techniques and their expertise in handling people, may be very helpful here; sometimes a combined visit from social worker and doctor may tip the scales. It is emphasised that this is only done where it is agreed that it would be genuinely in the patient's interest to make this move.

If an old person has doubts about residential homes, a visit may be arranged by the local authority social worker; or a limited day-care arrangement may be tried. In these ways some of the barriers may be broken down and groundless fears removed.

There is a sliding scale of charges up to a maximum determined by the local authority (based on the expenses of running all the homes in its area). The amount paid depends on one's means. A pensioner without capital, or with savings of under £800[1] pays only the minimum charge, which is the amount of the pension less £1.20 a week. This leaves the pensioner an effective £1.20 each week for pocket money. If an old person has no pension and cannot pay the minimum charge and manage to retain £1.20 a week pocket money, he may claim a supplementary pension. (This figure of £1.20 is due to be increased from October, 1972.)

Most Social Services Departments can arrange *temporary* admission to their homes to allow an old person's family to take a holiday or have a well-earned rest. If the old person is in need of nursing care or medical attention, such a "holiday admission" should be arranged with the local hospital geriatric department. All requests for holiday admissions should be made well in advance, prefer-

[1] If in receipt of more than one pension, this figure is reduced to £300.

ably when the relatives book their holiday several months before departure. These dates are guaranteed and the holiday can be anticipated and enjoyed without anxiety about the arrangements for the care of the elderly person.

Last-minute requests are almost certain to be refused since the homes and the hospitals can allocate only a small proportion of their beds for this type of admission.

21. *Special housing.* Apart from flats and bungalows built specially for elderly tenants, Housing Departments are increasingly providing "warden-controlled accommodation" for old people. This is also known as Sheltered Housing or, most recently, Grouped Dwellings. Such schemes consist of houses, flats, flatlets, or rooms in houses, which are purpose-built or specially adapted for the elderly. They are usually grouped together, and a resident warden is employed to keep a general watch over the residents. Her duties may range from cleaning to social work, and her precise role tends to vary in different schemes. But she is contactable by a bell or intercom in each old person's dwelling, and the confidence this inspires in the residents is the measure of the great value of this form of housing for the elderly.

It must be noted that the Warden is not a Home Help, nor is she expected to perform nursing duties. She is in effect a "good neighbour" who will help out in emergencies, and an important part of that help may well consist of marshalling aid from the appropriate sources— e.g. local authority, general practitioner and/or voluntary bodies.

Residents need to be basically independent when they move into such a dwelling and at one time would have been thought ideal for local authority residential homes.

Modern informed thought prefers to place them where possible in grouped dwellings, leaving the residential home places for the less fit, more frail old people in need of care and attention.

These dwelling schemes provided by Housing Departments do not come under the aegis of the Social Services Department—nor of the medical profession. A letter from a doctor may help in placing an old person or married couple in one of these schemes, if there are true medical grounds for supporting the application.

In thinking about the selection of tenants for grouped housing, it should be borne in mind that these dwellings are intended to be the permanent homes of those tenants, and frequent moves to other accommodation are undesirable. Thus, even though a tenant becomes physically or mentally frail over the years, she retains her flat or bungalow and supporting services are brought in as neccessary—just as if she were living in "unsheltered" accommodation.

In schemes which have been in existence for some time a high proportion of tenants may be in this frail state, and when vacancies arise it is inevitable (and fair) that fitter and possibly less elderly persons should be selected to help to "balance" the grouped community. In accordance with the remarks on the Warden's role, made above, relatives must try to appreciate the true nature of the Warden's functions. She may have to be a "good neighbour" to thirty to sixty old people and must not be thought of as a substitute for other people whose direct involvement with the resident would be more appropriate—relatives, friends, statutory and voluntary services. For this reason the age-range and general fitness of the grouped scheme must be viewed as a whole, and a balance maintained.

22. *A new act.* Under the Chronically Sick and Disabled Persons Act 1970 local authorities are responsible for informing themselves of the numbers and needs of the disabled in their area. Social Services Departments are asked to provide or help to provide for disabled persons, registered as substantially and permanently handicapped, a wide range of personal, recreational, educational and environmental facilities.

Such facilities include many of those mentioned earlier, such as meals-on-wheels, home help, equipment and adaptations to the home, outings and holiday arrangements, books, radio, television and telephone. In addition, help with travel, or more specialised equipment may also be available.

Housing authorities are encouraged to develop special accommodation for the disabled, and public buildings must develop—or be built with—access facilities, including access to toilets and parking, for the disabled.

Fuller details are set out in a leaflet issued by the Central Council for the Disabled, 34 Eccleston Square, London S.W.1, and the National Fund for Research into Crippling Diseases, Vincent House, Vincent Square, London S.W.1, but advice on a particular situation may be obtained from local authority Social Services Departments or from the voluntary Old People's Welfare Committees.

It should perhaps be stressed that this Act has been in operation little more than a year. Its provisions cannot all be fully implemented at once, and there may well be deficiencies in different areas. The delays are partly due to the current reorganisation of the administration of Local Authority services along the lines recommended in the recent Seebohm report (see Chapter 6).

VOLUNTARY SERVICES

There are many voluntary bodies which supplement and complement the statutory services for the elderly. It is fortunate that this is so, for local authority services alone would be unable to meet the demand, and the efforts of voluntary organisations—and of relatives and neighbours let it be emphasised—are of vital importance in maintaining many elderly people in the community. Voluntary organisations provide services such as the following:

Meals-on-wheels are usually organised by the W.R.V.S., in co-operation with the local authority.

Old people's clubs. At first these were afternoon clubs but many now take old people for whole days, as with day centres. They provide social facilities and encourage good neighbourliness. Many provide lunch and/or tea. Various activities are available in these clubs, such as keep-fit classes, drama groups, country dancing, singing, handicrafts, photography and so on. Some of these may be classes run by the local education authority. Outings and holidays may be arranged.

Such clubs provide a valuable method of "bringing out" old people, which often means bringing out the best in them. Not only do they keep active and alert but they find ways of being of use to others, and may take part in friendly visiting of frail, ill, or recently bereaved old people at home, and in various activities within the club.

There is often friendly rivalry between clubs, as seen in competitions and exhibitions.

Such clubs are run by local old people's welfare organisations, the W.R.V.S., the Red Cross, and religious organisations. Some are run by the National Federation of Old Age Pensions Associations.

Clubs based on parishes and held, say, in church halls, are invaluable in large cities, where decentralisation of the facilities is essential.

Disabled persons' clubs. Whilst old people's clubs are for healthy as well as frail old people, disabled persons' clubs are specifically for handicapped persons, of any age. There may be specially adapted transport available. Special-purpose clubs may exist—e.g. for the deaf (of all ages); or for those recovering from mental breakdown (contact the National Association for Mental Health, 39 Queen Anne Street, London W1 M 0AJ).

Friendly visiting. Loneliness may often be prevented by visits from volunteers who will offer company and perhaps lend a hand with household tasks. Such visits are especially useful at times of bereavement, but are best continued as regular visits, to establish a good personal relationship. Voluntary visiting schemes are run by old people's welfare organisations, tenants' associations, Toc H, International Voluntary Service, Women's Institutes, churches, youth clubs and the various young people's groups such as Task Force, Community Service Volunteers, Youth Action, or the Young Volunteer Force Foundation. Old people may be given a card to place in their window if they want to be visited or if they run into difficulties—for example, the "Fish Scheme" and related schemes where a particular symbol is used as a sign that help is required.

Good neighbour services may be provided by the voluntary organisations mentioned in paragraph 4, as well as the local authority. Some of these bodies will also help with house decoration, gardening, etc.

Chiropody may be provided at clubs or at home.

Equipment loans. The British Red Cross Society will lend nursing equipment, wheelchairs, walking aids, etc., in addition to the similar service provided by local authorities and hospitals (see above). Other voluntary bodies may also assist in this direction.

Holiday schemes. Various types of holidays may be organised by voluntary bodies, ranging from "convalescent" holidays to holidays arranged by a club for its members.

Boarding-out schemes. Volunteers may find households prepared to "foster" an old person, i.e. to accept him as a paying guest, but ideally to absorb him into the life of the family as far as possible. Most schemes are run by Old People's Welfare organisations or Councils of Social Service. The local authority may give financial support to the scheme and a supplementary pension may be available to pay the boarding charges in cases of need. The "boarding out officer" who matches up the households and the guests will keep in touch with both and will deal with any problems which may arise—especially if the boarding arrangement cannot be continued due to ill-health or other difficulties.

Unfortunately, perhaps, such schemes are all too rare at present. It is quite likely that many old people could fill a "grandparent" rôle in a family with whom they are boarded, to the mutual benefit of all concerned. This rather revolutionary idea calls for much more serious thought by society as a whole.

Special Housing Associations. These are increasing in number. An example is the Abbeyfield Society (Headquarters: 22 Nottingham Place, London, W.1) which acquires private houses and converts them into bed-sitting rooms, each house with a resident housekeeper and communal dining facilities. The houses are acquired in areas which the residents know or would wish to live in. Residents have their own furniture and belongings and are encouraged to do what they can for themselves and for each other. The whole aim is to provide a homely atmosphere, comfort, security and friendship.

There are over 300 local Abbeyfield Societies in the United Kingdom, owning 500 houses. Charges depend on the house and the area: each house is intended to be self-supporting.

Other associations sponsor purpose-built accommodation for the elderly, e.g. the Hanover Housing Association, 168d High Street, Egham, Surrey. This is a non-profit-making organisation set up by the National Corporation for the Care of Old People and it covers the United Kingdom. Each scheme (flats or bungalows) has a resident warden and bell-system.

In some housing schemes a capital contribution is required.

Almshouses. Many old almshouses remain in use, but are being progressively modernised or rebuilt.

Voluntary organisations' homes. These homes are usually small, and situated mainly in areas of high population and residential districts. Most are run by religious bodies of various denominations, although they may not be exclusive. The Salvation Army and Church Army run such homes.

Various welfare organisations also provide homes for the elderly, as well as homes for people with specific handicaps such as blindness: the main ones are Old People's Welfare organisations, Councils of Social Service, several housing associations, national charities and professional and trade organisations.

These homes have to be registered with the local authority. There is likely to be a waiting-list, as with local authority homes, and it is as well to plan ahead, as far as possible, and if the possibility of requiring a place in a home is foreseen—however remotely—the old person's name should be advanced for inclusion on the list at the earliest possible moment. By the time the vacancy arises, one may be in a better position to judge if it is wanted: it can always be refused, which will cause no problem since there are always others waiting. On the other hand, the sudden realisation that a place in a home is advisable leads to problems, because having to wait a year or two from that point onwards can cause great hardship to an old person and her family and neighbours. So, as always with old people—plan ahead.

In case of financial need, the local authority may be able to pay the residence charges, or part of them, under a contractual arrangement.

Privately Financed Services

Private homes. Like voluntary homes, private residential homes for the elderly must be registered with the local authority. Unlike voluntary homes, private homes are run for profit. Their standards vary greatly, and preliminary inspection is advised before making definite arrangements.

Special attention should be paid to the layout, especially the provision of W.C.s and bathroom, steps and stairs, provision of a lift to upper floors, fire precautions, attitudes of staff to residents and visitors, quality and quantity of food provided and freedom for the residents.

Charges may not be fully inclusive; they will vary from about £14 a week to over £40 a week. High cost does not guarantee satisfaction, but very low cost must imply some limitation of facilities.

Nursing homes. Similar considerations apply to nursing homes. Because they must employ qualified residential nursing staff, and should provide night staff, their charges naturally are on a higher scale than private residential homes, and usually start at about £22 a week. In many instances, of course, they are only required for temporary stays but, in some, frail or handicapped old persons are in residence.

Private nursing at home. There are private nursing agencies which can provide temporary or permanent nurses. These agencies tend to be found mainly in the South of England, where there is a high concentration of retired persons, and in London. They must be registered with local authorities.

Some nursing help may be available in London through the Elderly Invalids Fund (10 Fleet Street, London, E.C.4) but demand for such assistance is always greater than its supply.

Other Help Available

Financial help for relatives. Many relatives do sterling work in caring for their elderly dependents, with little financial assistance or reward. In a sense, they are sub-sidising the local authority services, whereas the opposite arrangement would make more sense and represent social justice—the relatives should be subsidised. The cost, related to the possible alternative of prolonged or unneces-sary hospitalisation, would be modest and economically intelligent.

In some other countries a relative's allowance may be paid in such circumstances, and its size is not inconsider-able.

In the United Kingdom, apart from modest Income Tax concessions, it has not hitherto been the practice to pay relatives for caring for their disabled elderly folk although, as stated earlier, relatives may sometimes be eligible for payment as Home Helps. However, from 6 December 1971, an Attendance Allowance may now be paid to a person who cares for a totally dependent relative. The condition for the payment of this allowance is that the patient must be severely disabled, needing day and night care continuously and must have been in this condi-tion for at least six months (conditions which may be somewhat relaxed in the future). The value of this allow-ance is £4.80 a week, tax free, but this is due to rise to £5.40 in October 1972. The Department of Health and Social Security has issued a leaflet on this subject which may be obtained, with a claim form, from its local offices directly or by application in a pre-paid envelope, obtain-able from post offices.

National Suggestions Centre. This organisation was set up in 1968, supported by private and state-owned com-panies, the Department of Health and Social Security, and King Edward's Hospital Fund, to receive ideas from the public as consumers, and several projects have resulted which are aimed at improving conditions for the elderly.

Further information is available from the Centre at 18 Victoria Park Square, London, E.2.

In the hospital service

Many old people who become ill are sent to hospital. Of those with medical—as distinct from surgical—problems, some are seen by general physicians and may enter general medical wards. Others will be referred by their family doctors to a consultant physician in geriatric medicine—geriatrician, for short—and may enter a ward of the geriatric department. This may be situated, in the more enlightened or more fortunate places, in the main general hospital, but is sometimes in a separate smaller hospital.

These segregated hospital buildings are often old, often former workhouses, and the stigma of their inglorious past is likely to persist into the present day! But do not be deceived by appearances: there is new wine in those old bottles. Most geriatric departments are nowadays practising very progressive medical care of old people, and some of the best work is done in some of the oldest buildings. In such places there have usually been considerable attempts made to upgrade the interiors to a more modern standard, but it is common experience that this exercise can swallow up large sums of money and still leave so much which is unsatisfactory that it is preferable to rebuild wherever possible. The public, it seems, finds it hard to reconcile modern rehabilitative effort with the old workhouse buildings.

Happily, there is now an increasing tendency to provide new purpose-built wards and buildings for geriatrics, often within the district general hospital, so that problems of the physical fabric of the buildings, so misleading to the layman, are being progressively solved.

The geriatrician is a fully-trained general physician who has chosen to specialise in the medical care of old people. He leads a team of junior doctors, nurses, physiotherapists, occupational therapists, speech therapists, medical social workers, liaison district nurses or health visitors and perhaps liaison local authority social workers, chiropodists and possibly other ancillary helpers. This team aims to evaluate the problems of each old person who comes to the geriatric department, and tries to see each patient as a whole person in his total environment. Apart from the medical aspects of the case, full attention is paid to psychological, social and economic factors.

A programme of investigation and treatment is planned for each patient according to his needs and a pragmatic view is taken of the chances of success in rehabilitating the patient and in influencing—where necessary—his environment. In drawing up this programme, an optimistic attitude is adopted whenever possible, for unjustified pessimism is a great hindrance in dealing with old people. (Readers who have read Part I of this book will readily understand this point.)

Thus the geriatric team is well-placed to obtain the best possible results for elderly patients, and its aim is to return the patient to his home whenever possible. Relatives and neighbours should realise that the patient may be much improved when he leaves the geriatric department, and his home may have been modified in some ways, so that a new situation exists which may work far better than in the days prior to admission. Much of the resistance sometimes offered to a patient's discharge comes from relatives who fail to grasp this point, or who have been so over-burdened by the original state of affairs that they cannot bring themselves to consider that the situation has been, or ever could be, ameliorated.

The geriatric team is much concerned with functional assessment of its patients. Apart from diagnosis and treatment, it seeks to establish the functional ability of each patient in terms of daily living activities—including getting out of bed, washing, dressing, cooking, feeding and using the lavatory. The geriatric department is equipped with a "trial flat", with a mock-up bedroom and a real kitchen, in which to assess and re-train the patient. Even after such rehearsals, discharges from the geriatric department are acknowledged to be trial discharges. All necessary support will be arranged at home, in terms of equipment, home adaptations and social props, but if the patient fails to cope he may be re-admitted for re-assessment and further rehabilitative effort. Why should there be such failures? Clearly because the gap between the sheltered environment of a hospital and the hard facts of living alone or having to cope for oneself can be too great for some patients.

In this connection, the Day Hospital may play an invaluable part, which will be considered in section 4, to follow.

Community Services of the Hospital Geriatric Department

(1) *Re-admission.* Geriatric departments try to "guarantee" their service by offering re-admission of patients whose discharge from that department has been followed by relapse. Wherever possible such re-admission will be arranged with a minimum of delay. However, as usual with hospital re-admissions, these arrangements

must be made via the family doctor. The knowledge that a "failed" discharge will lead to speedy assistance once more from the geriatric department helps to bolster the morale of patients who may doubt their own capabilities; in practice relatively few patients require early re-admission and the numbers have lessened with the advent of Day Hospitals.

(2) *Intermittent admission.* In genuine cases of need, the geriatric department will consider regular intermittent admission of an old person. In this way the hospital shares the care of some elderly invalids with their relatives. Dates of admission and discharge are pre-arranged and—failing emergencies—are guaranteed by both parties. The scheme may involve six weeks in and six weeks out—which is the way it started—or it may be more flexible in order to fit into the needs of the individual case.

(3) *Holidays.* Where relatives can offer more continuous care to the elderly, but need to be assured of an opportunity to take a holiday secure in the knowledge that the old person will be well looked after whilst they are away, the geriatric department can again be of help.

The conditions are, as in (2), that the patient must need nursing care and/or medical treatment, and that dates must be guaranteed by both parties.

Early booking is as essential for the stay in hospital as it is for the actual holiday for the relatives. Last minute requests usually lead to disappointment.

(4) *The Day Hospital.* Day Hospital care was started by psychiatrists in Russia in the 1930s. Following the opening of the first psychiatric Day Hospital in this country in 1952 the idea was taken up by pioneer geriatricians. The first geriatric Day Hospital opened in Oxford in 1958. The value of this form of help for ill or disabled old people was quickly appreciated, and many geriatric

Day Hospitals now exist throughout the United Kingdom. The Department of Health and Social Security emphasises the increasing need for Day Care in coping with the increasing numbers of elderly people in the community who need medical assistance. The term "Day Care" includes not only Day Hospitals but also Day Centres, run by the local authority or voluntary organisations, as described above.

The Day Hospital is a bridge between in-patient care and a patient's independent existence at home. It provides six or more hours of medical and nursing care, rehabilitation, and social facilities daily.

There are several ways in which the Day Hospital helps to restore, preserve and develop physical and social competence in the elderly. Thus the Day Hospital:

Prevents unnecessary admissions to hospital beds by providing investigation and treatment in cases where the "bed-and-breakfast" or "hotel" element of hospital care is not required—for instance, where relatives can cope after they return from work, and overnight

Allows treatment to begin before a planned admission as an inpatient

Allows earlier discharge from hospital beds whilst affording continued opportunities for treatment

Allows the discharge from hospital wards of some patients who would otherwise become long-stay, either permanently or whilst awaiting residential accommodation

Maintains improvement after discharge from the ward and helps prevent relapse, thus reducing the need for frequent re-admission

Relieves strain on relatives and neighbours during the day and allows breadwinners to continue at work

Encourages mixing of in-patients and out-patients, with mutually beneficial results

Provides such important treatments as chiropody, bathing, bowel-control and hairdressing

Ensures a good hot meal and other refreshments

Provides companionship, stimulation, and activities for the lonely, apathetic, and self-neglectful

Facilitates resettlement in the community by softening the impact of sudden discharge from in-patient care to the greater rigours of independent existence.

From this long list of functions it can be seen that the Day Hospital is a vital link in the chain of continuing comprehensive medical care of the elderly, which is the keystone of geriatric medical practice.

Note that the Day Hospital is *not* a Day Centre. Day Centres have been described earlier—they are run by local authorities and voluntary bodies to provide social and diversional activities and to encourage good nutrition for the elderly. The Day Hospital is intended to provide in addition a wide range of medical and nursing treatments, and these comprise its prime function. It is best regarded as a type of hospital ward without sleeping accommodation for the night.

Like any hospital ward, it must achieve a turnover of patients if it is to continue to function smoothly and to offer its benefits to the maximum number of patients.

A patient may start attending daily (i.e. each weekday, since few Day Hospitals are open at weekends) or on two or three days a week; gradually the frequency of attendance is decreased to one day per week, and then the patient is discharged. Some patients only require to attend once weekly from the outset.

The final severance from Day Hospital attendance may be difficult for certain patients who become emotionally attached, and in these, as well as in those who will benefit from continued companionship and diversional activity, transfer to a local authority Day Centre is advisable.

For the mentally ill. Mental illness in the elderly may often be managed in the community—at home, in hostels or residential homes, in psychiatric out-patient departments of general hospitals, or in day centres (for the elderly or for the mentally handicapped) or Day Hospitals. Everything depends on the type of illness and the particular provisions for community care of the mentally ill in the area of the country concerned. Some mental hospitals have a special department for old people, which may be known as a psychogeriatric department.

Occasionally such a department may exist in a geriatric hospital, but for anything other than an acute confusional state due to a physical illness—such as pneumonia or urinary infection—the mental hospital is the more appropriate site for such a unit. Geriatric wards are intended for old people whose illnesses are predominantly physical, and psychogeriatric wards are for those with predominantly mental symptoms.

The Dept. of Health & Social Security now suggests the development of acute psychogeriatric units for assessment purposes only, within geriatric departments. Such assessment work, in patients with mixed physical and mental symptoms, is carried out all the time in the assessment wards of all geriatric departments, and a separate unit is not always felt necessary by geriatricians.

The important point is that such units cannot hold patients for more than two to four weeks, and they must then be transferred elsewhere. By this time the mental symptoms have often cleared or come under control sufficiently to pemit the patient to return home, possibly with Day Care as continuing support. This Day Care may be given in special psychogeriatric day hospitals or centres where available, along the lines previously described. In other cases the control of mental symptoms still leaves considerable physical disability and the patient may then be appropriately transferred to an ordinary geriatric ward with a view to discharge home in due course.

The whole pattern of care for elderly patients in both geriatric and psychogeriatric units is aimed at the shortest possible stay. The idea of long-stay beds (suggesting, in this context, permanent stay) is largely going out, and every effort is now made to find alternative ways of caring for the elderly. Living out one's days in a hospital ward is rarely a satisfactory way to spend one's last months or years. The public has come to terms with this development for it is a reality, and has to be faced by many patients and their relatives. It is especially important in the case of mental illness, for long-stay beds for the elderly in mental hospitals are being progressively reduced.

Improved community support is obviously essential to counteract the effects of this, although this is developing in a patchy way and some areas are more fortunate than others in the provisions being made to help keep the precarious old person at home.

Liaison between psychiatrists and geriatricians, and between hospitals and the social services, enable these comprehensive care schemes to be organised. Much assistance in liaison between hospital and community is provided by medical and psychiatric social workers, who also do a great deal to help patients and their relatives with individual problems.

Mental hospitals may also have liaison community nurses or health visitors attached to them, as for geriatric departments.

How to find help

It is regrettable that there is no single source of information and assistance which can cope with all problems concerning the elderly. Some such centralisation may come in the future as a Geriatric Advisory Centre, possibly based in a hospital geriatric department; but this seems a long way off.

At present, the initial approach is best made to the old person's *family doctor* .He will be pleased to give advice and suggest the channels which might be explored with advantage. In some instances a doctor's letter is required to obtain assistance—including *Home Help, district nurse, holidays,* referral to a *hospital geriatric department.* In other cases a doctor's letter may be of help in obtaining or hastening a favourable result (*residential accommodation, re-housing*).

For *local authority services,* contact the local office of the Social Services Department (look up the address in the telephone directory or ask in the post office or public library); occasionally an approach may more appropriately be made to the Health Department[1] (for *laundry service,* or *chiropody*), or the Housing Department (for *re-housing,* special warden-supervised *grouped dwellings,*

[1] The guiding rule is that personal social services and mental health services come under the Social Services Department, other health and medically-related services under the Health Department.

or *adaptations* to the home—though this last is usually channelled through the Social Services Department first).

Home adaptations may also be undertaken by voluntary agencies, such as the British Red Cross Society (9 Grosvenor Crescent, London, S.W.1., or local branches).

Equipment loans may be obtained via the Social Services Department or the British Red Cross Society. Ideas about aids and gadgets may be obtained from publications of the British Red Cross Society, the Central Council for the Disabled (34 Eccleston Square, London, S.W.1) and the Disabled Living Foundation (346 Kensington High Street, London, W.14; Tel: (01) 602 2491); see also Chapter 7. The first two of these organisations can also supply information on *holidays for the disabled*.

Chiropody may be obtained via local authority or voluntary body clinics. Ask at the local Health Department or Old People's Welfare Council. Occasionally it may be possible to obtain from these sources domiciliary chiropody at the home of a housebound old person. To find a private chiropodist consult the Society of Chiropodists (8 Wimpole Street, London W1M 8BX).

Library service. Ask at the local public library if there is a mobile library service which will call at the house. If there is no mobile service, voluntary organisations can usually find someone to change books for a housebound person. Large-print book are available.

Blind services. Contact the local authority Social Services Department. A social worker from that department can arrange for the teaching of braille or Moon, and can give details of the many services available for the blind, and arrange inclusion on the Blind Register.

Books and periodicals in braille or Moon can be sent post-free, and the National Library for the Blind (35 Great

Smith Street, London, S.W.1, and 5 St. John Street, Manchester, 3) provides such a free lending service. Talking Books are available from the British Talking Book Service for the Blind (Nuffield Library, Mount Pleasant, Wembley, Middlesex) who will also lend (for a nominal rental) a playback machine. The rental can be paid, in cases of need, by the Social Services Department.

The Royal National Institute for the Blind (224 Great Portland Street, London W1N 6AA) also provides numerous services for the blind, from white sticks to rehabilitation courses.

A fit elderly blind person who can cope with a guide-dog may apply to the Guide Dogs for the Blind Association (83-89 Uxbridge Road, Ealing, London, W.5). The applicant will be assessed by a trainer and, if able to undertake a tough course of training, may be allocated a dog. It is unusual, however, for a dog to be given to anyone who goes blind after 60 years of age.

Deafness. A social worker from the local Social Services Department is a useful source of information about help for the deaf. The Royal National Institute for the Deaf (105 Gower Street, London, W.C.1) will provide advice about the problems of the deaf, including literature on hearing aids; a free test of a hearing aid is also available through this organisation. However, satisfactory aids[1]—including their servicing—can be offered via hospital Ear, Nose and Throat Departments which have Hearing Aid Centres in various situations associated with district general hospitals. Access is via the family doctor.

Special aids to help with the telephone, TV and radio, and various gadgets using lights rather than sounds, are

[1] N.H.S. hearing aids tend to be large and somewhat cumbersome. A movement is afoot to try to obtain smaller, more discreet aids under the N.H.S., such as those currently available to the private purchaser.

described in a booklet published by the Royal National Institute for the Deaf.

Clubs for deaf people (of all ages) are run by the British Association for the Hard of Hearing (contact the Honorary Secretary, Briarfield, Syke Ings, Iver, Bucks), and this Association also provides helpful literature.

Day Centres. Apply to the local Social Services Department and to the Old People's Welfare Council; it may be convenient to approach religious organisations directly. The National Federation of Old Age Pensions Associations (address below) may be able to help locate clubs.

For *residential accommodation* the approach should be made via the same channels as for Day Centres.

For old people's dwellings and *sheltered housing (grouped dwellings)* an approach should be made to the local authority Housing Department.

Voluntary Services are co-ordinated by local Old People's Welfare Committees or Councils, and these are organised under the aegis of Age Concern—formerly known as the National Old People's Welfare Council. Enquiries started here may save much time and trouble in tracking down particular services provided by individual voluntary bodies—e.g., location of clubs and homes, loan of particular items of equipment, provision of visitors, "Good Neighbours", and night-sitters, holidays and boarding-out schemes. Alternatively, one can try the local Council of Social Service or Citizens' Advice Bureau.

Useful addresses

Age Concern
55 Gower Street, London, W.C.1

British Red Cross Society
9 Grosvenor Crescent, London, S.W.1 (consult Telephone Directory for local branches)

Community Service Volunteers
28 Commercial Street, London, E.1, and 29 Queen Street, Edinburgh, 2

International Voluntary Service
91 High Street, Harlesden, London, N.W.10

National Association for Mental Health
39 Queen Anne Street, London W1M 0AJ

National Council of Social Service
26 Bedford Square, London WC1B 3HU

National Federation of Old Age Pensions Associations
91 Preston New Road, Blackburn, Lancs.

National Federation of Women's Institutes
39 Eccleston Street, London, S.W.1

Spastics Society
12 Park Crescent, London W1N 4EQ

Task Force (for London)
Clifford House, Edith Villas, London, W.14

Toc H
41 Trinity Square, London, E.C.3

Women's Royal Voluntary Services
17 Old Park Lane, London W1Y 4AJ

Young Volunteer Force
Abbey House, 2-8 Victoria Street, London, S.W.1

Voluntary bodies' homes must be registered with the local Social Services Department which will allow inspection of the register. They may be more directly located via the Old People's Welfare Councils, Councils of Social Service, or by direct approach to religious organisations such as the Salvation Army, Church Army, Society of Friends, Jewish Welfare Board, Methodist Homes for the Aged and Catholic Churches. Useful addresses under this section are:

The Salvation Army
101 Queen Victoria Street, London, E.C.4

The Church Army
185 Marylebone Road, London, N.W.1

The Society of Friends
Friends' House, Euston Road, London, N.W.1

The Jewish Welfare Board
74a Charlotte Street, London W1P 2AH

Methodist Homes for the Aged
1 Central Buildings, Matthew Parker Street, London, S.W.1

National Council of Social Service (see list above)

Women's Royal Voluntary Services (see list above)

The *R.N.I.B.* and *R.N.I.D.*, mentioned earlier, may be able to provide information about voluntary homes for the blind and deaf respectively.

Specific organisations such as *Housing Associations,* and professional or trade bodies may provide homes for their members.

The British Legion (49 Pall Mall, London, S.W.1) runs several homes for ex-servicemen.

Cheshire Homes (Cheshire Foundation Homes for the Sick, 7 Market Mews, London, W.1) take disabled persons of all ages but are intended mainly for younger persons. Various (unfortunately named) "Homes for Incurables" also tend to select younger patients.

Useful publications: The *Catholic Directory*, published annually, lists homes for Catholics. The *Charities Digest*, is published annually by the Family Welfare Association (Denison House, 296 Vauxhall Bridge Road, London, S.W.1). This gives information about major national charities home and trade or professional organisations' homes.

Housing associations. Ask at the Old People's Welfare Council, Council for Social Service, or Citizens' Advice Bureau. The National Association of Almshouses (Billingbear Lodge, Wokingham, Berks RG11 5RU) lists almshouses according to county in its yearbook. Some charities and trade and professional organisations have set up housing schemes for the retired. The *Charities Digest* (see above) may help locate these. Many religious bodies and some local churches provide them too. Further help may be obtained from the Elderly Invalids Fund, (10 Fleet Street, London, E.C.4). The Abbeyfield Society has its headquarters at 22 Nottingham Place, London, W.1. The Hanover Housing Association is based at 168d High Street, Egham, Surrey. For those with some small capital and income, Mutual Households Association Ltd. (41 Kingsway, London, W.C.2) convert fine old country houses into flats for retired people, and the Institute of Directors' Retirement Advisory Bureau (10 Belgrave Square, London, S.W.1) may also be of help.

Private residential homes. Consult the register at the local Social Services Department and double-check with the local Old People's Welfare Council, Council of Social Service or Citizens' Advice Bureau. These voluntary organisations may have more details about the homes which will help in trying to choose one. If in difficulties try the Elderly Invalids Fund.

Nursing homes. The local Health Department keeps a register of nursing homes. Again the voluntary bodies and the Elderly Invalids Fund may supplement the information obtained.

Private nurses. There are various private nursing agencies. Consult the Yellow Pages in the Telephone Directory.

Variations in Scotland. Details of Scottish social services may be obtained from the Scottish Council of Social Services, 10 Alva Street, Edinburgh EH2 4QH, or from local authority health and social services departments in Scotland.

3

Towards the End of
the Road

"Men fear death, as children fear to go in
the dark; and as that natural fear in children
is increased with tales, so is the other."—
Sir Francis Bacon

Facing the inevitable

DEATH is one of the few remaining taboos in our society
today. It is, apparently, not to be talked of. Yet just as we
are all born so must we die; death is part of life and a good
death is a fitting end to a good life. The manner in which
we die is important: ideally it should be peaceful and
comfortable, physically and mentally; and not prolonged.
It should be free of fear and guilt. To some degree, re-
ligion and its ministers may play an important part here,
and some people show an increase in being religious
in later life or when death approaches.

In many cases, however, good nursing and good medical
care are also required to achieve a good death. Old
people are, inevitably, nearer to death than are young
people. When they fall ill, old people are more at risk of
dying than are young people. If an illness is seen to be
ending the patient's life, there is still work to be done to
ensure that the end is peaceful and comfortable. Good
nursing is the keynote, but does not imply the need for
admission to hospital. Old people should, whenever poss-

ible, die at home in familiar surroundings and surrounded by the familiar faces of relatives and friends.

Removal to hospital at this time is a regrettable upheaval at a time when minimal disturbance is required. However, there will inevitably be some patients who cannot for one reason or another be cared for at home, and they may then be admitted to hospital or nursing home. The district general hospital may take the patient, but many dying elderly patients will be referred to geriatric departments. If there is a need for admission, they will be welcomed, and will be given devoted nursing care. The doctors will endeavour to see that meddlesome investigations and unnecessary treatment procedures are avoided, and will prescribe drugs to abolish pain, suppress cough, ensure sleep, and so on. When such care of the dying leads to the good death which is aimed at, the team and the relatives should feel satisfaction at a successful outcome. For when death is inevitable, a *good* death means success for all concerned.

Hostels for the dying

These are homes and hostels which specialise in care for the dying patient, and, contrary to what might be expected, the atmosphere in them is cheerful and not morbid, happy rather than sad, peaceful rather than disturbed. Relatives are encouraged to become involved in helping out; doctors and nurses make a point of spending time with the patients in conversation and activities as well as their more formal duties; there are flowers and bright curtains and furnishings. This all adds up to a positive approach which is of enormous benefit to the patients, who can talk out their fears and fantasies in a calm atmosphere.

Just as there is often fear of death, so may a dying patient fear to enter such a home—but once there the fear is rapidly dispelled and, when the end comes, the patient usually dies a calm and content person.

Euthanasia

Euthanasia means, literally, a "good death". *It means nothing more.* Unfortunately, however, it is widely used in the sense of "mercy killing"—a putting to death by deliberate intent, and the term then acquires a completely different significance.

Voluntary euthanasia. This term is used to indicate that an adult person of sound mind, whose life is ending with much suffering, should be able to choose between an easy death and a hard one and to obtain medical aid in implementing that choice. There would appear to be a narrow margin between this and suicide—in both cases the subject deserts the world of his own volition. Most religious authorities oppose this on the grounds that man is assigned a place in the world by God, and may not determine his own life span and so violate the sixth Commandment.

Historically, pagan writers and many philosophers through the ages have favoured voluntary euthanasia. Plato (fourth century B.C.) supported it and so did Sir Thomas More (a devout Catholic) in "Utopia", requiring *ad hoc* authorisation in each case by the priest, and equating this with the Will of God for the person concerned.

Voluntary euthanasia has never been legalised in Great Britain, although serious support for its legalisation in this country dates from 1873. The Voluntary Euthanasia Legalisation Society was formed in 1935, with Lord

Moynihan as its President. It was supported by several eminent men—including H. G. Wells, Harold Laski, G. M. Trevelyan—and some clergymen. A Bill obtained a second reading in the House of Lords in 1936 but was opposed by the famous physicians Lord Dawson and Lord Horder, as well as by the Archbishop of Canterbury, and it was dropped. However, it was recommended that attention should be paid to the quality as well as the quantity of life, and this is still the concern of all those working on behalf of the elderly, for whom one aims to "add life to their years", rather than merely adding years to life.

Another Bill to legalise voluntary euthanasia was rejected by the Lords in 1969, but further efforts in this direction seem certain to be made.

It is therefore worth considering some of the arguments often put forward for and against voluntary euthanasia:

FOR

Compassion: Suffering should be minimised; man should not be refused what we would not deny to animals.

Free Will: Man has a right to take his own life or ask for it to be ended, if his suffering is a burden to him and to his relatives—and suicide has been legal since 1961.

Strain on relatives: of watching a patient die slowly and painfully.

Legal position: at present unsatisfactory.

AGAINST

Compassion: Whilst pain and suffering should—and often can—be relieved, deliberate killing is wrong and ignores

124

moral and ethical values. Compassion should not be man-centred, but based on man's relationship to God.

Free Will: Man is not a free agent, but influenced by, and involved with, relatives, friends, subconscious motives, climate of opinion, social forces and emotional disturbances. His ability to choose may be impaired due to his disease[1]—if psychologically predisposed to suicide he might desire euthanasia more easily when ill. In some cases the patient may have requested euthanasia—should it become necessary—prior to his actual illness, only to change his mind when the reality draws near. This kind of ambivalence has been noted by an eminent psychiatrist in many dying patients—they may change their minds from day to day. In this connection, another eminent psychiatrist, especially interested in suicide, points out that patients who have previously attempted suicide and failed may subsequently lead useful lives; when these individuals eventually die naturally, they do not die better (more resignedly or stoically) than those who never had suicidal tendencies. In other words, personality may change; and this applies especially to those with long-term incurable illnesses. The fact that such a person has signed a form some long time previously requesting euthanasia, is therefore inadequate protection even though the right to change one's mind is always present.

Strain on relatives: This argument can be used in an opposite way—doubts, guilt-feelings, and other anxieties may plague relatives who agree to or actively encourage euthanasia for the patient.

Legal position: Although suicide is legal, "accessories" to the deed are punishable. This places "advisers" in a

[1] The patient is sometimes supposed to be both sane and "crazed with pain" at the same time!

dubious legal position. But legalisation of voluntary
euthanasia would lead to the risk of persuasion of the
patient by others—a real risk, however honourable the
motive—or too ready an acceptance of the idea by the
patient, to "reduce the burden on others"; and there would
also be the need for doctors to adopt the role of "execu-
tioners".

Many doctors might agree in principle to voluntary
euthanasia, but fewer would be prepared to carry it out
for their patients. A doctor's prime duty is to preserve
life; if attending a patient with a terminal illness he will
endeavour to relieve pain and suffering and thus assist in
achieving a gentle and easy death, but the idea of deliberately killing—even in circumstances of terminal illness—
is repugnant to most doctors. The doctor's vocation is to
cure sometimes, to relieve often, to comfort always.
Imagine too, the undermining of confidence a patient
would feel for a doctor who might be instrumental in
taking his life on any one of his visits.

Proponents of voluntary euthanasia suggest various safe-
guards to ensure that errors are avoided and that no undue
pressures are exerted on the patient or his relatives. Apart
from the disconcerting formalities these would require, the
organisation of the actual euthanasia procedure would
appear to present administrative problems.

Several authorities with extensive experience of the
dying patient have contributed to the literature on this
subject. Here are three relevant quotations for the case
against euthanasia:

DR. CICELY SAUNDERS: "We believe that proper care and
control of distress among these patients *can* and *should*
prevent them from even reaching that desperate place

where they ask that steps should be taken to hasten the end of unendurable suffering."

A. D. WEISMANN and T. P. HACKETT: "The proper management of terminal illness has a positive purpose and a standard of success that includes more than the mere absence of pain and complaint. The aim is to enable the patient to go on living throughout this part of his life as himself and not as 'an uncomplaining residue'."

TWYCROSS: Terminal illness is not a negative and humiliating experience for doctor, relatives and patients if handled well. Spiritual values may be very important and life may be ended with pride and dignity. Voluntary euthanasia is an undignified way out of what has become —through neglect or ignorance—an undignified situation.

Involuntary euthanasia. One of the arguments often put forward against legalising voluntary euthanasia is the risk that *in*voluntary euthanasia might follow rather readily. This means the putting to death of individuals or groups of people without their consent, people who are considered to be "undesirable" on one pretext or another. Clearly this has the ring of Nazism, and is abhorrent to most of the civilised world. G. K. Chesterton expressed the fear in his opposition to euthanasia: "Some are proposing what is called euthanasia; at present only a proposal for killing those who are a nuisance to themselves, but soon to be applied to those who are a nuisance to other people." Who are the people who would be at risk if involuntary euthanasia were permitted? Once the concept is accepted that there is such a thing as a life not worthy to be lived, many groups of underprivileged people might be included—the mentally handicapped, chronically sick, severely crippled, old and demented, socially undesirable or unproductive, and then, as in Nazi thought, the ideologically and racially unwanted. This is the wedge principle—once an exception is made or a precedent created the door is open for the entry of bigger and wider groups.

Most proponents of voluntary euthanasia insist that they reject the concept of involuntary euthanasia, but many of them have made statements which would appear to contradict this. It would seem that demented senile persons would be an early target for this exercise.

A Summing up. Medicine, like politics, is the art of the possible. It is *possible* for doctors to kill patients. But it is also the art of the ethical, and no ethical problem is more difficult than euthanasia. The issue revolves about whether it is more compassionate to shorten a distressed life already near its end or to keep it in peace until its natural close. The fact that we sometimes fail to achieve such peace does not necessarily mean that we should switch to euthanasia; and we should sometimes fail there, too, for many possible reasons.

Doctors are trained in the tradition that they are trustees of individual human life. It would be sad indeed to see this tradition overthrown.

Far better to improve our education. Doctors, medical students, and nurses must be taught how to deal with dying patients, to keep them in sufficient physical, mental and spiritual comfort to prevent them from even thinking of asking for their lives to be ended prematurely and deliberately. The public must also be taught to understand more about death and dying and to stop this subject being a taboo never to be mentioned but often feared.

This is a far better answer to the problem than voluntary euthanasia. Let us revert to our definition of euthanasia as "a good death"—or, if you prefer, "a gentle and easy death". Of course the medical profession should help its dying patients to achieve this—but it should not have to kill them to make the point.

4

A Look to the Future

"Gauge a country's prosperity by its treatment of the aged."—Nathan Bratzla

THE increasing development of all aspects of community services will undoubtedly be the keystone of the pattern of care of the elderly in the future. The aim will be to keep every old person at home if at all possible, and the ways in which this can be done have already been described in Chapter 2 of this book. Whereas many of the services are at present patchy, they will clearly need to be developed to a more consistently high standard throughout the country. With the proposed reorganisation of the National Health Service the creation of "Community Physicians" to replace Medical Officers of Health may help in further co-ordinating the development of these local authority services.

In this connection, the more effective application of the Chronically Sick and Disabled Person's Act 1970, will facilitate the necessary improvements. Needless to say, financial considerations are the major problems here, and much depends on what increases a community will accept in the rates.

Financial help for supporting relatives could be improved with advantage to the individuals, the community, and the State.

Boarding-out arrangements could probably be greatly expanded and comprehensively developed. Many able-

131

bodied middle aged and elderly persons live in accommodation which is far more spacious than they require. With suitable encouragement and financial incentives they might well be prepared to accept an old person into their home; preferably as "part of the family".

In addition an old person could act in a grandparent role if boarding with a suitable family and this could be of mutual benefit.

Clearly such schemes could be hazardous if compatibilities were not carefully checked, but they have been shown to work in areas where they have been tried—in Colchester, for instance.

Prevention better than cure. As explained earlier, great emphasis will be placed on prevention of disability and disease. Health visitors, family doctors, social workers and geriatric consultative or health clinics will help to uncover much occult disease, and day centres and day hospitals will help prevent breakdowns. Screening for various diseases such as diabetes, glaucoma, cancer and tuberculosis, is a well-established technique now as applied to communities. The prevention of accidents in the home and the street offers much scope for the future.

Research. There is enormous scope for research in all aspects of ageing and old age. This research has been slow to develop and spread in the United Kingdom, but there are now signs that it is gathering momentum.

Some biologists believe that prolongation of the human life-span will become a reality in the future; clearly we shall have to equip ourselves with better techniques for coping in (and with) old age if this is to occur. With a prolongation of life we need a prolongation of the period of vigour; otherwise we shall surely gain little in the long run.

The increase in total population would be small compared to the problem of high birth-rates. The problem of world over-population must be tackled by improved birth-control and not by holding back progress in understanding and combating ageing.

Education. There is a great need for education in matters concerning old age. Public education is of vital importance in this respect. A recent television play included a statement from a young layabout that he did not relish being beaten up as he did not want "to land up in a geriatric hospital"! This misconception on the part of the scriptwriter could have widespread harmful effects on a gullible audience. *The true facts about geriatric hospitals, outlined in this book, are easy to grasp and worth knowing by everyone who has, or may expect to have, dealings with an elderly relative, neighbour or friend, and indeed by old people themselves.* Awareness of the facilities available to make the lives of old people healthier, happier and more active and useful is of benefit to the whole community.

Education of professional workers is also necessary—whether social worker, nurse or doctor. All need a thorough grounding in the problems and their amelioration, and (in the author's experience) in *the need for optimism in dealing with the elderly.*

Not least one must ensure that politicians understand the problems of the elderly, and the ways in which these problems may be tackled with particular reference to the development of the various key services and the plugging of gaps therein. There is a welcome feeling that this is now happening to some extent, but the efforts will need intensifying and must be kept up if we are, as a nation, to fulfil our obligations to our senior citizens.

5

Some Typical Situations:

Their management and mis-management

Trivial causes of big problems. Aged 89, Mrs. A. lived alone and had severe untreated corns. She found it very painful to walk, and stopped going out of her flat. Soon she found it too uncomfortable to get about the flat and took first to an armchair all day and then to bed, where she felt much more comfortable. It gradually become too much trouble to get out to the lavatory, and she used a bucket by the bed. But soon she found she could not get to it quickly enough and she began to wet the bed. She was by now very constipated and then developed loose motions over which she had no adequate control. The skin of her back and buttocks become wet and dirty and sore, and broke down. She was admitted as an emergency to a geriatric ward and rehabilitated. The bowel was cleared and with the resumption of walking her urinary problems cleared up. But the healing of her ulcerated skin on her back and buttocks took several months. The chiropodist dealt with her corns in fifteen minutes!

Mrs. B. aged 72. This lady lost her lower denture at the Day Hospital, though how she managed to do this was never very clear. During the next two weeks she developed recurrent blistering of her right great toe and her walking—never very steady—deteriorated alarmingly. Just when it was thought that she would have to be admitted to the ward it was found that her missing denture was in the toe of her right slipper! (Another moral of this story is that old people should wear proper shoes when walking—they provide better support to the feet and are less likely to flop about and contribute to accidental falling.)

Mrs. C., aged 82, fell and broke her right wrist. It was set at the local hospital and a plaster-of-Paris cast applied. She was quite unable to manage at home on her own and became neglectful of herself and her house, and very depressed. Home help, meals-on-wheels, and a district nurse to help her take a bath made all the difference— but they should have been arranged right at the start without waiting for her to get into difficulties.

Drug hazards. Mrs. D. This 81-year-old lady had been "anaemic all her life" (many patients say this; fewer are correct). In recent years she had been tried on different iron preparations by her doctor. What he did not know was that she kept the surplus in each bottle whenever a new preparation was prescribed. She was visited by a district nurse because of severe constipation. The nurse found that Mrs. D. had four different iron preparations in her flat, and was taking them all at the same time "to get quicker results". She was lucky, for the results could have been far worse than constipation. (When a drug is stopped or changed by the doctor all previous tablets or medicines no longer needed should be thrown down the W.C. Hoarding of drugs can lead to subsequent confusion, as seen in the next example.)

At 74, Mr. E. developed a cough and became increasingly confused, especially at night. He began to break up his flat, threw his furniture out, and disturbed the neighbours. The doctor gave him antibiotics for his chest infection, and might have settled rapidly but for the fact that he unearthed some sleeping tablets in a drawer and tried those. They were barbiturates, which are often badly tolerated by old people, in whom they may cause restlessness and confusion instead of sleep. They had been prescribed for him years ago by another doctor. Mr. E. was admitted to a geriatric ward to tide over this crisis and within two days was his usual self and able to return home.

At 81 Miss F. used to cycle round town and was very fit. She developed appendicitis and sailed through the operation without turning a hair. After some days she became a little confused at night and was given a tranquilliser. She became worse and was given more tranquilliser, and then a sedative, and then a sleeping pill. By now thoroughly maniacal, she was seen as an urgency by a geriatrician. He stopped all drugs and called for careful nursing only, keeping the lights on and reassuring the delirious patient. She settled down by next day and never looked back, and was soon cycling again. (In old people, drugs should be given in small doses, and one can often do more good by stopping drugs altogether than by switching from one to another; but it may be necessary to tide the patient over till the effects of previously-administered drugs have worn off.)

Dogged independence. Mrs. G. This old lady was 101 when she was admitted to a geriatric ward after a fall. She had not injured herself but lost confidence and "gone off her feet". She lived alone and insisted on getting going again so that she could return home. She soon began walking again with the aid of a walking-frame, and returned home, with the "social props" organised for her—home help, meals-on-wheels, district nurse, visitors from Task Force.

Mrs. H. lived alone (aged 72) in a tiny, dark basement flat in utmost squalor. She allowed no one to see her bedroom. Her living room-cum-kitchen-cum-washroom had an old sink (cold water only) and an older gas cooker, some furniture and a great deal of dirt. She herself was equally dirt-ingrained. Physically she appeared remarkably well, but she was anxious and hysterical, and announced that she was going to have a stroke and so she would never go out. She had a devoted home help, who did far more than was expected of her, but could still make little impression on the place. Meals-on-wheels were sent in daily, but were probably given to the cat, which was as fat, sleek and healthy-looking as the patient was thin, shabby and drawn. She was clearly neglecting herself in every way, but there was no medical indication for hospital admission. She refused to consider going into a residential home because she would not be parted from the cat. She also refused Day Centre attendance for the same reason. The Welfare Officer knew her well and kept an eye on her, but could offer little more in the way of help. The patient mistrusted strangers and the main hope lay in establishing a personal relationship with her over a period of time, and eventually persuading her to accept a place in a residential home—or first, perhaps, in a psycho-geriatric hostel. Day Centre attendance would be of great value to such a person, if only it could once be started.

Mrs. J. lives alone but does not cope very well. Aged 76, Mrs. J. tends to leave empty kettles on the lighted gas-ring of her cooker, to have heaters full on in confined spaces, and to show forgetfulness in various other ways.

Clearly she is a danger to herself and her neighbours. Yet she is a very charming old lady who refuses any suggestion of going into a residential home. She is not physically ill and does not need a bed in a general or geriatric hospital. She is not mentally ill in the true sense and does not need a bed in a psychiatric hospital. She must be kept in the community somehow. Ideally she would be placed in a residential home for the mentally frail, where such exists. She would probably also manage quite well in an ordinary residential home. But if she refuses to go it is impossible to force her. Perhaps a visit to see such a home might change her mind, and some local authority Social Workers will arrange this. The first line of action, however, may well be attendance at a Day Centre, preferably a psycho-geriatric one, or a Day Hospital, for retraining purposes in "daily living activities". (It is not possible—or desirable —to remove all muddled old people to an institution. Admittedly this means that some risks will have to be accepted, and of these the risk of fire is the most serious. But attendance at Day Centres, visits by relatives, neighbours, friendly visitors, home helps, district nurses, etc. all help to reduce the risk by providing periods of supervision. It may be all that can be offered until the old person agrees to enter a home.)

False alarm. Miss K, aged 86, complained of inability to hold her water for six months. She passed water frequently by day and night. Because she tended to have slightly swollen ankles, she was being treated with a drug which made her pass more water than normally. When this drug was stopped her urine output reverted to normal, the frequency decreased, and she was able to control her waterworks again. Her ankles did not swell to any greater extent and she felt very well. She was mentally alert and physically well preserved. The quality of her life was altered by curing her "incontinence". She was greatly relieved.

Relative's (undeserved) guilt. Mrs. L., aged 88, was being treated in a hospital geriatric department for immobility due to arthritis and obesity. The obesity was considerable and was aggravating her difficulty in walking. Ordinary dieting failed and she was placed on a "crash" diet which was very strict. Her daughter, a highly articulate spinster of some fame in her chosen career, complained to the Board of Governors about the "inhuman" treatment of her mother. After several interviews with the consultant physician she began to admit that she felt an acute sense of guilt at being unable to offer her mother adequate care and she realised that this was being converted into anger at the hospital for instituting an "uncomfortable" treatment for her mother. She soon came to appreciate all the efforts being made for Mrs. L., who lost weight successfully, became mobile once again and entered a residential home in due course. It should be noted that Mrs. L. had never at any time complained about her treatment. (Old people are only put on strict diets if it is vitally important for them, since it is difficult to change their habits at this time of life. Guilt in relatives is often projected as anger against those most trying to help. It can often be assuaged by sympathetic handling.)

Emotional blackmail. Mrs. M., aged 67, had a long history of depressive illness, treated at various times throughout her life. She was "spoilt" by her husband, who waited upon her and left her little to do in the house. After his death she proved a great burden for her unmarried daughter, who had to go out to work to make ends meet. Mrs. M. remained depressed most of the time, and very weepy and slowed-up. She insisted that she could not possibly be left alone, and her daughter was forced to give up her job. However, after a period of treatment as an inpatient (in a geriatric ward in this instance, for she had some minor physical disabilities as well, which were dealt with at the same time) she became cheerful and responsive and showed much more initiative. She began attending the Day Hospital prior to discharge and continued daily attendances as a day patient after discharge from the ward. Her daughter (disbelievingly at first) was thus enabled to resume her work and the situation was transformed thereafter.

Some elderly people use this sort of "emotional blackmail" to keep control over relatives at home. The latter may not only have to give up work but also be afraid to leave the house in case the old person runs into trouble. It is all too easy to be beaten by this stick; such a situation may well be avoided or remedied by intervention by a doctor or social worker.

A Note on the Organisation and Reorganisation of Health and Personal Social Services

FOR a quarter of a century the United Kingdom has had a National Health Service organised as a tripartite structure of hospital, general practitioner and local authority services. The administrative divisions between these branches of the National Health Service have led to difficulties and illogicalities, and an attempt is now being made to re-plan the N.H.S. in a more logical manner to coincide with the reorganisation of local government. Both these re-structured organisations are due to become operative in 1974, with co-terminous boundaries in most areas.

Meanwhile, reorganisation of the local authority health and welfare services has already got under way along the lines recommended by the Seebohm report of 1968. The new arrangement is to create Departments of Social Services, which will include Welfare Services for children, the elderly, and the physically handicapped, and also take over some of the functions previously belonging to the Health Departments (especially the Home Help Service and mental health social work) in order to group personal social services under one administrative department as far as possible. Nursing services and health visiting will remain with the Health Departments, however. The term "Welfare Department" is therefore obsolete—or more realistically, obsolescent.

7

Aids to Daily Living

"A.D.L." comprises an important aspect of assessment and treatment of handicapped patients, and is therefore relevant to many people, especially those living alone.

In geriatric departments much emphasis is placed on this aspect of rehabilitation, since a person's ability to function independently must be seen to be satisfactory before he or she is plunged straight from the shelter of a hospital to the more exposed situation of living at home, possibly alone, and perhaps with few friends or relatives nearby. Even the best personal social services cannot make up for inability to perform natural bodily functions, for example, and any difficulties in this direction must be dealt with before a patient can be expected to return to the community, otherwise breakdown in the home situation is inevitable.

Similarly, it is often essential for the patient to be able to get into and out of bed alone, or perhaps with only minimal help from another person living in the same dwelling. Training by physiotherapists and occupational therapists can often restore this ability even if it has been lost temporarily due to illness or loss of confidence. Other such "basic" activities include washing, dressing, cooking, eating and so on—all things we take for granted until we find ourselves in difficulties coping with them when, for instance, we have an arm or a leg in plaster following a fracture.

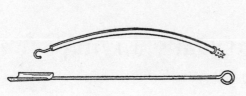

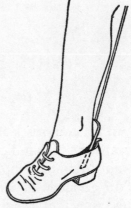

Dressing-stick (clothes-hanger, hook, and rubber thimble) and long-handled shoe-horn.

Long-handled shoe-horn in use. Note Elastic shoe lace.

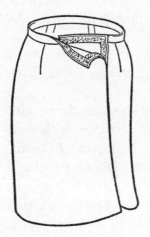

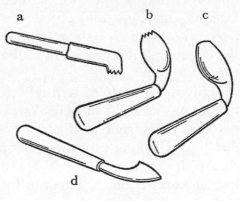

Wrap-around skirt with Velcro fastening at the front.

Cutlery for people who can use only one hand.

a, Nelson knife; b, c, d, "Manoy" cutlery.

Training can be undertaken in all these essential daily activities and deficiencies can be compensated for by special techniques and by gadgets and modifications to clothing and to the home.

It is worth considering some of these aids to daily living in more detail, as a little inventiveness and a small expenditure of time or money can bring large rewards to the disabled, restoring them to independence and incidentally effecting considerable economies to the National Health Service.

Dressing aids

A *stocking aid* is a long-handled gadget with a "gutter" at one end over which a stocking or sock may be slipped prior to applying it the foot and drawing it up the leg. An improvised version uses a rubber thimble on a stick.

By varying the length and shape of the stick a series of useful *dressing sticks* can be provided; one such handy gadget is made from a clothes hanger with a rubber thimble at one end and a hook at the other.

A long-handled shoe-horn and ready-tied elastic shoe-laces are also helpful in some cases.

Ties are available ready-tied with an elastic attachment to slip over the head and down to the neck.

Clothing design may be important in helping a disabled person to retain his or her independence—e.g. front-fastening clothes, wrap-around skirts, skirts with split backs and generous overlay flaps, the use of "Velcro" (a self-adhering material whose surface is made up of innumerable tiny nylon hooks which interlock and hold together) rather than buttons or the troublesome hooks and eyes for fastening.

The *helping-hand* is a well-known trigger-operated

device with jaws at the far end of a long stick which may be used for picking up objects without bending down. It may be improvised by attaching long handles to a clothes peg or two.

Cutlery may require modification for arthritic subjects who cannot hold an ordinary knife and fork. Handles, for instance, can be expanded to allow greater ease of gripping by using cycle handlebar grips.

Specially-designed cutlery may help in some cases—the patient with a paralysed hand may cope with feeding herself if a Nelson-knife is provided. This is a knife and fork combined into one implement—the end of the knife blade is curved upwards and ends in a series of prongs which can act as a fork when the knife is turned over. The use of this knife is not without risks, especially in an unsteady hand or where there is difficulty in bringing the fork-end accurately to the mouth; accidents may happen. Some occupational therapists prefer to use a Manoy knife, which has a fat handle and a short rocker-blade; this functions as a knife only, but when the food is cut by using it in the good hand, it can be exchanged for an ordinary fork. This eliminates most of the danger in cases where a Nelson-knife may seem risky.

Kitchen gadgets

For one-handed persons *non-slip mats* are invaluable. They may be bought or improvised by using a damp "Wettex" cloth. In this way plates, bowls, etc. can be placed securely on the table or working-surface despite an inability to hold them with one hand whilst cutting or mixing with the good hand.

A *one-handed potato-peeler* is simply made from a flat piece of wood with a few vertical spikes. The under-

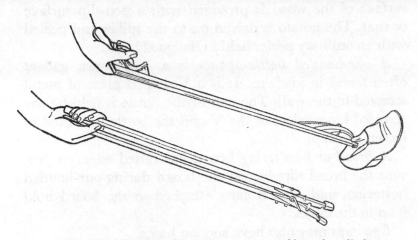

The "Helping Hand"—trigger-operated long-handled gripping device for picking up objects without the need to bend down.
Also shown is an improvised long-handled grip using a clothes-peg and two lengths of wood.

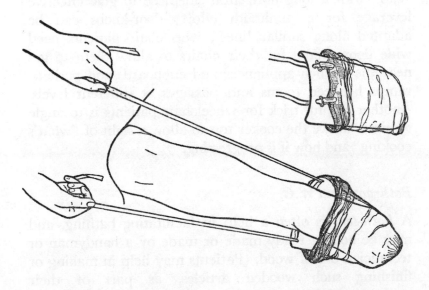

Polythene stocking-aid in use. Front and back views.

149

surface of the wood is provided with a non-slip surface or mat. The potato is driven on to the spikes and peeled with an ordinary peeler held in the good hand.

A one-handed bottle-opener is a well-known gadget often found in kitchens. It is a V-shaped piece of metal screwed to the wall. The cap of the bottle is held by the serrated inner edges of the V and the bottle is twisted to loosen the cap.

A bread-and-buttering board has raised edges to prevent the bread slipping off the board during one-handed buttering, and suction caps attached to the board hold it on to the table.

Egg cups may also have suction bases.

Other points to note in kitchens adapted for disabled patients include the provision of continuous work-surfaces to avoid unnecessary carrying; modifications to sink taps to facilitate their use (for instance, fitting on a wooden "cap" with a long horizontal sidepiece to give effective leverage for a minimum effort; door-knobs can be adapted along similar lines); wheelchair patients need wide doors, room for their chairs to allow them to get near the kitchen appliances and cupboards and perhaps ramps between rooms and passages at different levels. Another helpful trick for wheelchair patients is to angle a mirror above the cooker top to allow a sight of "what's cooking" and how it is progressing.

Bathroom and W.C.

A bath-seat is often a help in facilitating bathing, and may be bought ready made or made by a handyman or technician out of wood. (Patients may help in making or finishing such wooden articles, as part of their occupational therapy.)

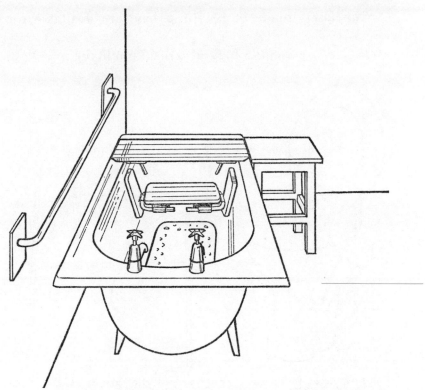

Bath aids: non-slip mat, two wooden bath-seats at different levels, stool level with higher bath-seat to allow person to slide on to (or off) latter.

Non-slip bath-mats are also important but unless they are pressed down really hard on the bottom of the bath they may fail to live up to their name and may indeed slip. A safer substitute is "Scotch Tread", an adhesive backed material which may be bought by the roll and stuck on to both the bath and the adjacent floor.

Hand-grips, strategically placed, may be needed for both the bath and the W.C.

Seat-raisers made of polypropylene are available for low W.C's.

W.C. chain-handles may also need modifying.

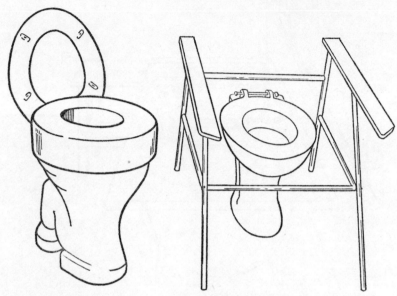

Polypropylene toilet-seat raise. No fixing necessary; easily removable.

Toilet aid—frame around toilet, with arms to facilitate standing from seated position. May be fixed; some are adjustable for height.

General mobility

Apart from the standard four-legged walking frames (Zimmer, Eedee, Carter, etc) there are various others which are of value in particular cases. Thus, two small wheels on the front two legs of a frame may facilitate walking in cases where difficulty is experienced in balancing and in alternately lifting the frame and putting it down again during walking. Such a "Rollator" is often of help in patients with Parkinsonism and in those who tend to fall backwards. There is danger in four-wheeled aids, as exemplified by the old lady who uses a child's push-chair or perambulator as a walking aid—"runaway" accidents may well occur. However, for use in the home, a four-wheeled trolley is provided by some Social Service Departments as this acts as a walking-aid as well as a practical help in fetching and carrying between rooms.

Some walking frames have "gutter" attachments for the forearms to rest in, for patients who cannot rely on gripping the frame handles. Others have crutch attachments to place in the armpits to help support the body weight; these special frames usually need front wheels.

Stroke patients who have lost the use of one hand and arm cannot easily cope with a walking frame, and they will be tried with one-handed aids—still with several "feet"—such as tripods or quadrupeds. Later, an ordinary walking-stick may be adequate; this should always have a rubber or composition ferrule at the end to prevent slipping. The length of the stick is important—the elbow should be slightly bent during its use but if it has to be very much bent the stick is too long.

Other subjects may benefit from a stick, including those with arthritis of the hip or knee. The stick should be used on the better side and put forward with the bad leg to increase support during use of the latter.

Bed aids

A bed of appropriate height should be available and may be borrowed, if necessary, from the local authority. It may have a pole at the bed head, with a "monkey-grip" handle to help a patient to manoeuvre in the bed and also to assist in getting into and out of bed. Hydraulic or electric hoists may be loaned by the local authority in suitable cases. To aid in sitting up in bed from a lying position one may tie a bandage or scarf to the foot of the bed.

Commodes should be of the same height as the bed or wheelchair. It is often necessary for the commode chair to have a detachable arm and side. "Chemical closets" are being tried in some areas where disposal of commode contents presents particular difficulties.

Armchairs should usually have the seat about 20 inches from the ground; in cases of difficulty in rising from the chair, an "ejector seat" may be useful.

Further Reading

General

Old Age Looks at Itself (Margery Fry) Age Concern, London.

Notes for Those Nearing and Over Sixty: Age Concern, London.

Understanding Old Age: (Ralph Emery) National Institute for Mental Health, London (1967).

Old Age: Office of Health Economics, London (1968).

Arrangements for Old Age: (Ed. Edith Rudinger) Consumers' Association (1970).

Health for Old Age: (Ed. Edith Rudinger) Consumers' Association (1970).

The Seven Ages of Man—collected articles from *New Society*, London (1970).

In the Service of Old Age (Anthony Whitehead) Penguin Books (1970).

Later Life, Geriatrics Today and Tomorrow (Ivor Felstein Penguin Books (1970).

Consumer's Guide to the British Social Services, 2nd. ed., (Phyllis Willmott) Penguin Books (1971).

Seventy Plus—A Handbook on Easier Living for the Elderly (Ruth Brandon) British Broadcasting Corporation (1972).

Services for the Elderly: National Corporation for the Care of Old People (1972).

Guide to the Social Services: Family Welfare Association (published annually).

Nutrition

Easy Cooking for One or Two (Louise Davies) Penguin Books (1972).

Retirement

Publications of the Pre-Retirement Association:
Aspects of Health in Preparation for Retirement.
Solving the Problems of Retirement (ed. H. B. Wright).
Pensioners in Search of a Job (F. le Gros Clark).

Other recommended books:

Inside Information on Pre-Retirement and Retirement (J. P. McErlean) Dickens Press.
Facing Retirement (A Country Doctor) Allen and Unwin, London (1964).
A Guide to Activities for Older People (M. G. Wallis) Elek Books Ltd., London (1970).
Retire and Enjoy It (C. Chisholm) Penguin Books.

Nursing

The Nursing of the Elderly Sick, 3rd ed. (T. N. Rudd) Faber, London (1960).
Looking After Old People at Home (Doreen Norton) National Council of Social Service, London (1962).
Nursing the Elderly (Mary A. Hodkinson) Pergamon Press, Oxford (1966).

Death

Dying (J. Hinton) Penguin Books (1967).
Bereavement: Studies of Grief in Adult Life. (C. Murray Parkes) Tavistock Publications London (1972).

Index

Accidents   54–7, 132, 136, 148
Accommodation 27, 42, 63, 64, 65,
    91–6, 97, 132, 138, 139, 140
Activities 51, 53, 71, 74, 89, 90, 97,
    98, 110, 145, 147
Adaptability, loss of   16, 29
Ageing, bodily changes in   29–31
    causes of   19–20
    of population   15, 23–9
    personality changes in   32–3
    process of   17–19
Aids to daily living 87, 114, 115,
    145–54
Almshouses   101, 119
Aloneness 27–9, 31, 107, 135, 137,
    138, 145
Anxiety   57, 63, 125, 138
Apathy   28, 64, 72, 110
Arteries, degeneration and
    diseases of 18, 22, 30, 42, 52
Arthritis 18, 34, 35, 39, 40, 52, 55,
    57, 85, 86, 148, 153
Attitudes, to old age   60–71

Balance, impaired   55, 58
Bath   83, 136, 150, 151
Bed, hazards of   38–9, 50, 66
    -pans   85
    -sitting rooms   95, 101
    -sores   38–9, 135
Bedding   40, 43, 84, 85
Beds   85, 153, 154
Behaviour, disorders of   38
Bereavement   28, 98, 99
Bladder, distended   38, 57
    function   40–5

Blind   88, 89, 102, 114–15, 118
Boarding-out schemes 100, 116, 131
Body temperature   31, 48
Bowels   38, 45–8, 57, 110, 135
Brain, damage causing incon-
    tinence   42, 44, 45
British Red Cross Society 87, 98,
    100, 113, 114
Bungalows, for the elderly   95–96

Cancer   22, 23, 84, 132
Cells, changes in function   20
Charges, for boarding-out   100
    for Home Helps   79
    for Meals-on-Wheels   81
    for private nursing homes   103
    for private residential homes 103
    for residential accommoda-
        tion (local authority,
        "Part III")   94
    for voluntary housing   101
    for voluntary residential
        homes   102
Chiropody 87, 90, 100, 110, 113, 114
Chronically sick   127–8
Chronically Sick & Disabled
    Persons Act (1970) 91, 97,
    131
Clothing   40, 42, 84, 146, 147
Clubs   89, 98–99, 100, 115, 116
Communication, problems   35–6
Community 27–9, 60, 68, 69–71, 93,
    96, 98, 108, 110, 111, 112,
    131, 132, 133, 139, 145
    services   77–104, 107, 112, 113,
    131, 138, 143–4, 145

157

Constipation 41, 45–8, 52, 53, 135
Corns 54, 135

Daily living activities 50–1, 107,
139, 145, 147
Day Centres 81, 87, 90, 98, 109,
110, 111, 116, 132, 138, 139
for mentally ill or handi-
capped 90, 111, 112, 139
Day hospital, geriatric 87, 88, 90,
107, 108–11, 132, 135, 139,
140
Deaf 31, 89, 99, 115, 118
Death, dying 20, 25, 26, 50,
121–9
Degeneration 18–19, 22, 34, 49
Delirium 37, 57, 137
Dementia 37, 45, 46, 128
Denture 135, 136
Department of Health &
Social Security 104, 108, 111
Depression 38, 57, 63, 111, 136,
140, 141
Diabetes 52, 54, 84, 132
Diarrhoea 45, 135
spurious 45, 135
Diet 51–2, 140
Disability 19, 28, 34, 58, 59, 61, 64,
68, 69, 83, 84, 90, 91, 97, 99,
104, 108, 112, 114, 118, 140,
147
Disease 18, 33–50, 83, 84, 132
District (Community) Nurses 29,
78, 82–3, 113, 136, 138, 139
liaison 106, 112–13
Dressing aids 146–8, 149
Drugs 37, 42, 43, 45, 46, 47, 49,
57, 58, 66, 122, 136, 137, 139

Education 71, 74, 83, 97, 128, 133
Emotions 63–4, 110–11, 125, 140
Equipment 85–7, 97, 107
loans 85, 87, 100, 114, 116
walking aids 85, 86
Euthanasia 123–9
Exercise 53
Eye diseases 31, 84

Faeces, 41, 45–8, 52, 53, 135, 136
Falls 51, 54–6, 66, 136, 137, 153
Fear 121, 122, 123, 127
Finances 71, 72, 73, 87, 89, 91, 94,
100, 101, 103, 104, 119, 131,
132
Flats, for the elderly 95–6
Forgetfulness 31, 32, 37, 138
Function, assessment of 106, 145
declining 18, 29
loss of reserves 18, 29, 34
psychological 32–3
recovery of 34
training 147
Functional ability 19, 51, 61, 107,
145

Gadgets 87, 89, 114, 115, 146–8
General practitioner 29, 70, 82, 88,
89, 92, 94, 95, 96, 105, 107,
113, 115, 132, 136, 141, 143
Geriatric department 39, 50, 66,
68, 70, 82, 83, 88, 92, 94,
105–13, 122, 133, 140, 145
community services 107–11
Geriatric medicine 18, 68, 105, 110
"Good neighbour" services 79, 95,
99–100, 116
Grandparents 33, 65, 100, 132
Grouped dwellings 78, 95–6, 101,
113, 116
Guilt 67, 68, 121, 125, 140

Handicapped 90, 91, 97, 103, 143
Handicraft classes 89
Health, and retirement 72–3
breakdown of 80, 100
in old age 19, 51–68
maintenance of 51–60
services (organisation and
re-organisation) 77–8, 143–4
Health clinics, for the elderly 59, 84,
87, 114, 132
Health Department (local
authority), 78, 82, 84, 113,
114, 119, 120, 143, 144
Health visitors, 59, 83–4, 132, 144

Health visitors—continued
liaison 106, 112–13
Hearing 31, 35, 89, 115
aids 89, 115
"Helping-hand" 147–8, 149
Hobbies 53, 72, 73, 74
Home adaptations 87, 97, 107, 113, 147, 150
Home helps 62, 78, 79–80, 95, 97, 104, 113, 136, 138, 139, 143
Home nursing 82–3, 144
private 103, 120
Homes, for the dying 122, 123
Homes, Old People's—*see* Residential Homes
Hostels, for the dying 122
for the mentally ill or frail (psychogeriatric) 111
Housebound 28, 81, 91, 114, 138
Housing Associations 101–2
Housing Department (local authority) 78, 95–6, 97, 113, 116
Hypothermia 48–50
Hysteria 138

Illness 33, 100, 145
mental—*see* Mental illness
long-term, incurable, 125
silent 35, 132
special hazards in the old 38–50
special problems in the old 33–50
terminal 126, 127
Immobility 40, 49, 54, 66
Incontinence 40–5, 46, 47, 84–5
Independence 51, 61, 70, 78, 80, 87, 91, 93, 95, 106–7, 109, 110, 137, 145, 147
Insomnia 57–8
Intellect, loss of 31, 32

Kidneys, degeneration 18
Kitchen, adaptations 150

Laundry service 84–5, 113
Library services 88, 114
Loneliness 27–8, 80, 99, 110

Longevity 21, 22
Lunch clubs 81, 98
Lungs 18, 32, 52

Meals-on-Wheels 62, 78, 80, 97, 98, 136, 138, 139
Medicines—*see* Drugs
Mental changes 31, 32–3, 36–8, 42–3, 44, 57
Mental Health 53, 72
services 78, 88–9, 90, 111
Mentally frail 92, 96
hostels 111
residential homes 111, 139
"Mercy-killing" 123

National Health Service 28, 77, 78, 143, 147
Night watching service 84, 116
Nurses, district—*see* District nurses
Nursing auxiliaries 82–3
Nursing, home—*see* Home nursing
Nursing homes, private 103, 119–20, 122
Nutrition 31, 51–3, 90, 98, 110, 140

Obesity 29, 52, 140
Occupational therapist 87, 90, 106, 145, 148
Old age 15, 16–7
attitudes to 60–71
bodily changes in 29–31
health in 51–68
illness in 33–51
maintenance of health in 51–60

Pain 31
Paralysed limbs 35, 148
Persecution, delusions of 38
Personality 32–3, 43, 62–4, 65, 70, 125
Physiotherapist 90, 106, 145
Pneumonia 26, 34, 47
Pre-retirement, attitude 72
courses 71–2

Prevention—*see also* Health, in
    old age, Health clinics,
    screening
  by district nurses   82
  by health visitors   83
  of bedsores   39
  of constipation   46–8
  of contractures   39–40
  of dehydration   46
  of hypothermia   49
  of urinary incontinence   40–5
Private residential homes 102–3, 119
Prostate gland, enlarged 31, 33, 41
Psychological changes 31, 32, 42–3

Rehabilitation 34, 50, 59, 68, 70, 71,
    89, 106, 107, 109, 115, 135,
    145
Rehousing, medical support for 113
Rejuvenation   21, 60
Residential homes 29, 67, 78, 88,
    91–5, 113, 116, 138, 139, 140
  private   102–3
  voluntary   101–2, 116, 117
Retirement 26, 28, 53, 71–5, 103,
    119

Screening, for ill-health 59, 84, 132
Seebohm report   77, 79, 143
Self-neglect   28, 110, 138
Senility   16–17, 128
Skin   29, 52, 82, 135
Sleep   52, 122
Smoking   52
Social problems   35
Social services 15, 28, 29, 77–104,
    112, 143–4, 145
  organisation and re-organi-
    sation 77–8, 97, 143–4
Social Services Department 59, 69,
    77, 78, 88, 90, 91, 92, 94, 96,
    97, 113, 114, 115, 116, 117,
    119, 120, 143, 153
Social workers 70, 71, 132, 133, 141
  Local authority 59, 69, 88–9, 92,
    94, 114, 115, 138, 139

  medical   106, 112
  mental health   88–9, 143
  psychiatric   112
Stroke 30, 34, 39, 40, 42, 49, 138,
    153
Suicide   123, 124, 125

Talking books   88, 89, 114–15
Telephone   91, 97, 115
Television   91, 97, 115, 133
Thrombosis, brain   22
  coronary   30
  heart   22
Transport (local authority) 83, 90,
    99
Travel   97
Tuberculosis   26, 132

Urine, bottle   41, 45, 85
  frequency   41, 57, 139
  incontinence 40–5, 46, 92, 135,
    139, 140
  infection   41
  obstruction   41
  retention with overflow 41, 42
  urgency   40, 41

Vigour, loss of   19, 53, 54
Vision   31, 35, 55
Visiting, friendly 99, 116, 138, 139
Voluntary bodies & Services 78,
    81, 87, 88, 89, 95, 96, 97,
    98–102, 110, 113, 114,
    116–9, 138

Walking aids 66, 85, 86, 137, 152–3
W.C.   40, 87, 150, 151, 152
Welfare Department — *see*
    Social Services Depart-
    ment
Welfare Officers — *see* Social
    workers (local authority)
Wheelchairs 85, 87, 100, 150, 154
Women's Royal Voluntary
    Service   81, 98
Work, during retirement 73–5